The Gaze of the Crucified Christ

The Gaze of the Crucified Christ

A Life, a Story, a Vision

PAULINE DIMECH

RESOURCE *Publications* · Eugene, Oregon

To all of us who love, laugh, and struggle.

Contents

Chapter 1   The Gaze of God   1

Chapter 2   A Life, a Story   4

Chapter 3   The Crucified Christ Gazes upon Me   51

Chapter 4   To Gaze at God   71

CHAPTER 1

The Gaze of God

How does one reduce a life into a book, especially when that life has seen almost six decades? How does one reduce into words the joy and the pain of being human? It is not at all possible to do that, but with treatment for cancer both behind me and before me, I want to leave something behind, something of my truest and deepest "self." Writers are often told that they need to keep their readership before their eyes, but I am not quite sure who would wish to read this book. All I know is that I have received a grace that has made me who I am, and that I intended to write this book many years ago, but never got down to it. What follows would seem to you like two books: one about my life, and one about a deep experience that I have had—that of the gaze of God. Although the connection between the two may not be obvious, the whole of life is always lived under God's gaze. It is just that we only get a glimpse of this in our lifetime, and sometimes we get a powerful reminder that helps us understand something of our past, our present, and our future.

Obviously, I am hoping that this book will be of interest to my family, friends, and acquaintances. Perhaps it will also interest the historian. There is a sense of history in this book, a sense of depth that only comes when one looks back and interprets the past from the eyes of someone still alive today. I hope that this book will not only provide pleasure and joy but also some understanding of what it means to be a baby girl born in the sixties in Malta: one who became a teenager during the seventies, a young adult during the eighties and nineties, and who then reached maturity after the turn of the third millennium. I am also hoping that this story will be of interest to women in the church. But, above all, I am hoping that this book will contribute something to those who are seeking to live a spiritual life, to those who desire to understand what their name is before God.

In my case, I found out my own name—or rather, my identity before God—at the age of thirty-four. I understood it to be connected to the gaze of God. When I was a child, one of the pictures that the catechists showed us to express the concept of divine omnipresence was that of an eye within a triangular form. The way it was explained to me was that God is a Trinity, and that he can always see where we are and what we are doing. The picture used to fill me with apprehension, if not fear. The poster with which I became familiar at an early age—as I started attending the catechetical center in Naxxar and was being prepared for the sacrament of Holy Communion at the age of six—seemed to be a judgmental, all-seeing look, one that filled me with unease. Knowing that God sees you everywhere and all the time may be a terrifying thought if you have the wrong concept of God.

But that is not the kind of gaze I experienced at the age of thirty-four, and it is not the kind of look I will be writing about. It was not at all what was manifested to me. This is not to say that I understood everything at that very moment when this private revelation occurred. You could say that the second half of my life has been a continuous attempt to understand what it means to be gazed upon by God, to understand what happens when one gazes upon God, and also to understand that there is a cost one has to pay if he or she wishes to stand before God's gaze.

The verb "to gaze" is generally defined as "to look steadily and intently." It could mean to stare, to look fixedly, to look vacantly, or to take a good look, typically in amazement, admiration, surprise, or thought. As a noun, the word "gaze" refers to a steady, intent look which reflects some kind of emotion. The gaze of my God is a fixed look. God's gaze upon us is always one of love, care, and pride in the person being gazed upon.

I have realized over time that I am not the only person for whom the gaze of God is deeply significant. There is a troupe of people that God seems to have chosen as his witnesses to this attribute of God: his gaze. Ignatius of Loyola was one of us. In the meditation on the incarnation, which involves the Trinity looking down on the world, we are asked to imagine God gazing down on us, and to imagine, along with God, that we can hear people laughing and crying, some shouting and screaming, some praying, others even cursing. It is a call to experience humanity in all its hues: in all its expressions, countenances, and protestations.

In my case, I was not called to experience the view of the universe from the point of view of God. Rather, I was asked to look at God in his most vulnerable moment, and to have him look at the core of my being. In my case, the gaze is that of the Crucified Christ—that is, of God on the cross at that very moment in history when he was vulnerable to the point of being abandoned. A moment when he seemed to have lost everything: his friendships, his health, his ability to perform miracles. A moment when he was wounded, abused, treated like dirt.

CHAPTER 2

A Life, a Story

MY LIFE, JUST LIKE that of everyone else, is a mystery. It started in another millennium in a village called Naxxar, on the island of Malta. The village has since grown into a town. I was born on Monday, May 20, 1963. My mother's name is Marianne (Marija Anna in Maltese), and my father is Peter (Pietru in Maltese), better known as Pietru ta' Frinu, a nickname that he got from his father.

My parents were married on 16 August 1959, and they held a simple reception at the Victory Band and Social Club situated in the Naxxar Square. I was born in the same house where my parents still live today, as I write this book. It is a house that represents the 1940s style in Malta, with a limestone facade, an arch over the main door, and a garage door alongside it. On the first floor, there is a window with a limestone frame and a traditional closed balcony, and there are stone balustrades on the roof terrace. The house was one of the first built on that street, constructed sometime in the 1940s. It was previously known as Buzjett Street, but is currently known as Triq in-Nutar Debono.

I was baptized on the Thursday of the same week in which I was born, and in the same church where whole generations of my ancestors were themselves baptized. The Naxxar parish church is dedicated to the Nativity of Mary—or, as it is better known, to Our Lady of Victories. It was the Feast of the Ascension the day when I was baptized. I was not the only child in the family. I have a brother who is slightly older than me, Francis, born in 1961. So, I was the second born. Another three followed: Reno in 1965, Victoria in 1969, and Christopher in 1971. So, in our family there were two girls and three boys. We were all baptized in the same parish church, although my mother was very devoted to Our Lady of the Way, an image of which was on display for veneration at the public chapel of the Jesuits in Loyola House, in Marquis Scicluna Street in Naxxar. My mother had had a spiritual experience in this chapel. When she was still childless she used to pray before this image, entreating Mary to give her the grace of a child. My mother is quite certain that she saw Our Lady handing over her son to her. Some time later, my mother found out that she was pregnant with my elder brother.

When I was still three or four years old, I used to go to St Monica school in Mosta. I remember very little of this time. But I remember the separation anxiety. I used to vomit every morning before I went to school. My anxiety disorder was there even at this young age. I still remember the Volkswagen Transporter van which used to pick us up from our home. I remember my anxiety at climbing the steps to my seat, and I remember my fear whenever the nun called me to write something on the blackboard. I do not remember who my teachers were, but I remember what my schoolbag looked like and smelt like: it was a red checkered bag which smelt of vomit. The gray hat that was part of the uniform is still stored at my parents' house somewhere, because my mother hardly throws anything away. My mom still stores clothing from our childhood in a packed wardrobe positioned up the last flight of stairs at our family home.

From Year 1 to Year 6,* I attended the government primary school in Naxxar. I remember all the teachers I had there: Ms. Vella taught me for two consecutive years. I then had Ms. Brincat in Year 3, Ms. Attard in Year 4, Ms. Schembri in Year 5, and Ms. Saliba in Year 6. They were all unmarried women who had found

---

* In Malta, we use Year 1 to Year 6 for the primary-school years, Form 1 till Form 5 for the secondary-school years, which are compulsory, and Sixth Form for those who take an academic direction after the compulsory-school years. There are other institutions after the compulsory-school years for those who wish to take the direction of art, science, or technology.

their maternal fulfillment as primary-school teachers. Ms. Vella was a member of the Society of Christian Doctrine, of which I became a member later on. The Society of Christian Doctrine (Latin: Societas Doctrinæ Christianæ; Italian: Società della Dottrina Cristiana; Maltese: Soċjetà Duttrina Nisranija; abbreviated SDC), is a society of Catholic lay volunteers, both men and women, which specializes in catechesis—that is, in the Christian faith formation of children, youths, and adults. It was established in Malta in March 1907 by George Preca, a Catholic priest who was canonized on June 3, 2007. It is better known as MUSEUM, which is an acronym that stands for *Magister, utinam sequatur Evangelium universus mundus*, which expresses Saint George Preca's prayer: "Divine Teacher, may the whole world follow the Gospel."[1] The Society has since spread to a number of other countries. I myself am very obliged to this Society. Not only did I receive my Catholic formation there, but it was also there that I met Christ, started reading the Bible, and had my first theological formation.

I still remember sitting for a test in Year 1 of primary school. The teacher was asked to choose the best student in the class, and I had to compete with a student called Ivan Attard, who later became an engineer. Ivan performed better than I did, but looking back, I realize that sitting for this test was already a huge achievement on my part. I came from a very humble background. My grandparents were practically illiterate, whereas this other student was from a professional family, with an aunt who was a teacher at the same school.

My worst year at primary school, in terms of achievement, was Year 5. The teacher was just too kind, and I remember being quite disruptive in class. I was usually—more often than not—among the top three students, but that year I was eleventh in class. My teacher in the final year was, in my opinion at the time, quite severe with me. The thing which bothered her, she confessed, was me having my hands under the table. I was always fascinated by my hands, and I used to fidget with my hands under the desk. She was always shouting at me because I was looking at my hands rather than at the blackboard. Later on, I did see her a couple of times, and I realized that what I had judged as an aversion toward me was really a personal interest in my success. I believe that she was a nun for a number of years.

I remember very little of what I learned, although I know that I hated mathematics and loved English. I was often complimented on the essays I wrote. One of the things I remember very clearly are the omega-3 fish-oil pills and the triangular milk pack that we were given daily. Another thing that I remember very clearly is listening to the religious broadcasts over the Rediffusion. Rediffusion (Malta) Limited was the name of the company which had been given the power and authority by the government of Malta to operate radio programs. It had the sole right of presenting news, views, and entertainment, either on sound radio or television, to the people of Malta. I also remember a small accident which I had right in front of the school. The garages which stand right in front of the elementary part of the school had been abandoned mid-construction. So, it was a construction zone for many years, and while waiting for the gates to open, my friends and I would play on this site, where limestone blocks had literally been tossed all over the place. It was an accident waiting to happen. I lost my front teeth there.

The headmistress we had at the girls' primary school, Ms. Maria Grazia Tanti, loved me until she died at the age of seventy-six in 1994. She always said that I was the first girl from Naxxar to do the BEd (Hons) at the University of Malta and the first female to be qualified with a teaching degree. I finished that course in 1987. I saw Ms. Tanti in her old age a number of times at the nursing home where she had retired. I used to visit another resident in the same nursing home in Attard, and I would drop in to see her.

My grandparents were farmers. They grew crops and kept livestock. As far as I can tell, all my ancestors were either farmers, or else they worked in construction, as stone carriers, as builders, or as contractors. One of my ancestors, Indri Calleja, has two streets named after him on the island: one in Birkirkara and one in San Gwann. My mother claims that Indri used to live at what is now the MSSP Oratory in Birkirkara and that he was responsible for the building of Villa Rosa in St Julians. Indri Calleja was probably the only figure of note in the whole of my family. He was my grandfather Nazzareno Micallef's grandfather.

As with every family, there are a number of narratives that run within the various generations of its history. And as always with these things, the truth is very difficult to establish. Ours has to do with Palazzo Parisio, formerly known as Scicluna Palace, which stands just across the road from the parish church in Naxxar. The Marquis Scicluna built the present palace between 1900 and 1907. The front and back facades were built in a modest art-nouveau style, and the interior in a Sicilian-baroque style. It is a beautiful palace, with an unassuming frontage but with huge halls decorated with gold leaf, a wonderful garden open to the public, and an amazing staircase.

It is believed that a hunting lodge was built on the spot in 1733 by Paolo Parisio. He had married, but died without having children. The narrative within my family did not go as far as establishing how the property came into the family. However, in 1856, it was already being used by my ancestors: the Micallef family. It has been said that the Micallef family claimed themselves as owners and declared themselves heirs without having any legal right to it. The narrative within the Micallef family was very different. My ancestors saw themselves as the rightful owners of the property. My own grandfather, Nazzareno Micallef, the son of Carmelo Micallef and MaryAnne, née Calleja, and grandson of Indri Calleja, was born there in 1899. For me and other members of my family, this was a case were the power of money won over the word of a poor farmer and villager. The Marquis Scicluna took my ancestors to court, and the entire land was released to the marquis on June 12, 1898, for the sum of £1500. A pittance, considering the size of the land.

My mother had a small field on the outskirts of Naxxar. We used to go there regularly. All my siblings, along with my mother. My own father had inherited his own piece of land from his own side of the family. But his was on the other side of Naxxar. Whereas my mother's was in Xwieki, my father's was just down what is known as the Telgħa ta' Alla u Ommu. We had a cart, and we used to pull it ourselves. The traffic must have been very minimal. This was in the 1970s. We had no self-consciousness. Today, I would not do that for any reward. We used to go to this field and play. I spent hours playing Ġenna-Infern. For this, you had to have a flower with many petals. These were generally wildflowers found in between rocks. You would pick one petal at a time and say "heaven," and then pick another and say "hell." It was a silly game dealing with serious eschatological realities. The name of the last petal would imply that that was where you were going to end up. There were other games similar to this where one would call out "love," "hate," "marriage," "adore." But the teens were generally the ones who played this, and I was still not into emotional games during the time we had this field.

My brother Reno had a section of this field which "belonged" to him. He used to till it himself. My mother used to sow and plant and just rejoice at whatever it was that grew. My father sometimes came with us to this field in Xwieki, but the visit often ended with an argument between my mother and my father. My father would pick vegetables or fruits when they had still not fully ripened, and my mother hated that. I did not really work the soil. I used to sit and observe the insects and just play in the shade of the carob tree.

In front of this field there was a quarry that was being used as a landfill. For us back then, it was a treasure trove. We never returned home without having picked something we liked from this junkyard. Whatever it was that we found would be carried on the cart or on an old stroller which we had and which was used instead of a shopping bag on wheels. My favorites were always the books and the comics. On one occasion, we found a huge quantity of books which had been rejected and thrown away by a school library. We carried everything that we could back home, about a kilometer and a half away. I believe that I read all the novels that were there. I do not think we have kept any of them, but at the time, they filled our library. We had not inherited a library from our ancestors as some of my contemporaries had. My grandmothers could hardly read. My grandfathers drew a cross where their signature should have been. My father was a laborer and my mother, a housewife. They were not ignorant people, but they had no academic background. My mom had only done primary school, whereas my dad had started going to a secondary school in Birkirkara, but soon gave up and went to work.

On another occasion, someone had thrown away old copies of the *Readers' Digest*, which we picked up, took home, and devoured.

For years, I used to spend some of my pocket money on getting the latest issue of the *Readers' Digest*, because I had gotten hooked. It helped that our teachers of English encouraged us to read it in order to improve our vocabulary. When I was in my teens, my mother bought the new revised edition of *Chambers's Encyclopedia*, published in 1973. She bought it from a door-to-door salesman. The complete set consisted of fifteen volumes, and I still remember her paying it in installments.Today, I have hundreds of books. What with my studies in education and my research about the spiritual life, catechesis, religious education, and theology, I now have so many resources! But, as a family unit, we started from scratch.

Once, we picked up a huge quantity of sewing-thread rolls. On another occasion, we found big files filled with letters of application for some professional job. The people who applied were all very qualified. I spent hours shifting through these pages, not recognizing any of the names but admiring their qualifications and achievements. There was no way at the time to find out who these people were. There was no internet or Facebook where you could just type in a name and find out about people. Furthermore, applications are generally sent online nowadays, but these letters of application were handwritten, some of them on beautiful writing paper. I am quite sorry that we threw these away in one of the number of cleansing Marie Kondo moments at my mom's house. My mother could be quite a hoarder, especially where fabric and sewing or craft materials are concerned.

As a child, I used to be so excited when my mother took us to Valletta. We would go by bus, of course. My mother must have been really courageous to take five of us on a bus. When Chris was three, my brother Francis was thirteen. I really remember very little about the shops we would visit. But I do remember that George Zammit, a spice shop, was always on the schedule. I hated it. My mother would spend what seemed like hours in there, and I could not stand the strong smell of curry. Another visit was to Aquilina Bookshop in Republic Street, or to Agius & Agius in South Street, two visits which I loved. The best thing was that we would always return with a book.

I guess you could say that we were a typical Maltese family. We were not poor, in the sense that we were not any worse off than others, although we did share a packet of Twistees, cutting it in half with a pair of scissors. Twistees is the iconic snack for the Maltese. My dad was a regular client at ix-Xallu, or the OK Caffe Bar, a popular bar which stood in Naxxar Square for most of my dad's life. My father left the house every afternoon around 5:00 p.m., went to this bar for tea, went to evening mass at 6:00 p.m., and then returned home with a box of Maltesers or a Cadbury bar. He probably brought home Desserta chocolate during the time that no foreign chocolates were allowed in. Thanks to Mintoff's economics, in the eighties you had to smuggle in non-Maltese chocolates if you wanted to taste anything besides Desserta.

Between 1964 and 1969, my father worked in Libya, and he had a very good salary. When I was young, I did not really enjoy the presence of my father. In the first year of his employment, he used to work three months in Libya and then come home for only five days. Later on, he used to work for one month there and then return to Malta for three weeks. When he came back for good—that is, when I was six years old—I was afraid of him, and I was shy in his presence. I used to see him as a huge person and as rough. I was a very anxious person and fragile, and I was frightened by his dominant personality. I remember one occasion when he beat me because I refused to do something that was expected of me and because I answered him back. I remember other occasions when he beat my brothers very harshly. I was afraid of his anger. Nowadays, I am no longer scared of him, and I can stand up to him. I should say that he never beat any of us once we had reached our teens. I know that he has a sensitive heart and that he is able to empathize and to have mercy, despite his rough appearance and the macho impression that he always gave. He is very much like a rhinoceros: he is scary, but he does not bite.

I always remember us having a television. I was still very young when my parents bought it. I remember my aunts coming to our house on a Saturday evening to watch the Black and White Minstrel Show. The same cannot be said where the telephone is concerned. We did not have a telephone when I was a child. My mother had to really push buttons in order to get a fixed telephone line. We waited for many years. I was over twenty years old when we finally got a telephone line. My mother also had to push buttons—and pull ropes—in order to get a colored television set. Today, it is difficult to imagine having to pay someone in order to get a service that other people already have access to. Corruption was rife back then, and people at all levels and in all roles used to get away with it.

It is amazing how many of my childhood memories are linked to TV programs. I remember watching Laurel and Hardy, Buster Keaton, and Charlie Chaplin on our black-and-white television. I remember watching *Star Trek* and *Space 1999*. I remember watching Shirley Temple. Movies were also an integral part of our childhood. My dad was quite an expert in 1950s films. I especially remember watching Jerry Lewis and Dean Martin. But John Wayne, Bing Crosby, Fred Astaire, and Frank Sinatra were also very popular with all of us.

I do not remember going to the movies except as a pupil at the Naxxar Primary School. We were taken to State Cinema in Triq Żenqa in Naxxar. I always loved it when we did. I do not remember the names of the movies that we watched, but I do remember certain scenes. In the meantime, the Jesuits used to organize a film show at St Aloysius in Birkirkara. It was there that we watched *Seven Brides for Seven Brothers* and *Oklahoma*, two musicals which I loved. A raffle would always follow the film, and there used to be some great gifts. On one occasion, my mother won a pair of knitted booties. It was so funny. After all the expensive gifts that were raffled, that was one of the few things that was left when she walked up onto the stage. We laughed all the way to Naxxar and for days after that. No offence to the person who knitted them, but it was such a comic anticlimax.

Music, laughter, and family life counted more than anything. As a family, we watched *Little House on the Prarie, Pippi Long Stockings, The Brady Bunch,* and *Man from Atlantis,* but I also loved *I Love Lucy, Green Acres, The Flying Nun, Mind your Language, Happy Days,* and *Allo Allo*. They were TV series that filled our lives with warmth and joy. As a family, we also enjoyed adventure and drama. The TV series *High Chaparral* was a case in point. We would look forward to the next episode as a family, and sit and watch it together. There was only one TV in the house, and there was no interactive TV, so you had to make sure that you were at home on time. On more festive occasions, we would watch musical shows or circus shows.

My father bought his first car when I was nine years old. We had an accident on our first outing, on the very first day. It was not my dad's fault. But we could easily have gotten seriously hurt with the way the accident happened. We were in Salina, driving along a curve in the direction of St Paul's Bay. I ended up with a cut on my lip.

My maternal grandmother had an enormous house in which we could create all sorts of adventures. I was very close to nanna Pawla, after whom I was named. I often slept at her house. She had a huge house with a huge garden and many rooms that were not used. When I was very young, she had a room for the chickens, one for the donkey and the sheep, and another for the rabbits. She had a kitchen and a dining room downstairs, which were never used, except by my cousins and I. The main door to the house was always open. Anyone could go in if they wanted. She had a seesaw in one of the rooms downstairs where we used to play. The seesaw was just a limestone brick with an unfinished wooden plank. My grandmother only used the upper floor of the house. The ground floor was for us. One of my aunts lived two doors down, and there were always cousins we could play with.

My grandfather, Żaren, or Nazzareno, was bedridden for fourteen years before he died at the age of eighty-four on March 18, 1984. In-nannu Żaren, as we used to call him, was a really handsome blue-eyed man who could easily have been mistaken for an aristocrat, although he was a farmer. Nanna Pawla was his carer for the whole time. As it happened, she died six months before he did, at the age of seventy-one. She was, as is evident from the dates, fourteen years his junior. Many people would associate her with her balcony. My grandparents had a balcony in their bedroom looking onto Main Street. Since nanna Pawla was housebound because of her husband, she used to stand on the balcony a lot and just talk to any passerby, whether it was a nun from the Dominican convent a few doors down, a student on his way to the Technical Institute, or even a dog. She died on 8 October 1983. I was doing my BEd (Hons) degree at the University of Malta at the time. I loved my grandparents a lot, in spite of the fact that they had received no formal education. They were courteous even though they were unschooled. My grandmother knew how to read and write a little. My grandfather only drew a cross when he was supposed to leave a signature. I used to spend a lot of time playing tombola with my grandmother, or else I would go through the old photos which she had inherited and which she treasured so much. I have no clue where these photos ended up after my grandparents' house was cleared in the eighties, but I would love to have one last look at them if I could. My grandmother always knew how everyone was related to everyone else. She was a real link to our past, because she knew our ancestors well and could make the connections. But most of that was lost when she died. Still, it was thanks to my grandmother Pawla that we learnt something about our family tree.

This grandmother had two sisters and a brother who never got married: Bertu, Roži, and Ċelest. Roži was a member of the MUSE-UM. She had a disability in her feet—clubfoot, to be exact. But she would leave the house everyday to go up the hill, across the main square in Naxxar, and to the MUSEUM in Castro Street—summer and winter. Roži was a simple, demure, and virtuous woman. Those who knew her would say that she had probably never even committed a venial sin. Was that at all possible? She was truly a good person. Her sister Ċelest died when I was in my thirties. She, too, was a holy woman, but she was also wise. We used to call them "iz-zija Ċelest" and "iz-zija Roži," and I continued to visit them in the nursing home where they retired until they died. I loved zija Ċelest to death when I was a girl. She used to take my brother Reno and myself to Għajn Riħana, where she had fields. We used to walk to Għajn Riħana from Naxxar, and we used to spend days in the fields there. I remember crying in my bed thinking that someday I would have to live without nanna Pawla and zija Ċelest. I used to think that it would be impossible to live without them. As it happened, God did not take them away from me until it had become possible for me to live without them. My heart still misses a beat when I go past their house, because I have such beautiful memories. My great aunts lived in Triq is-Salib, or Cross Street, whereas my grandparents lived in 102 Main Street. This was the street down which all the town's traditional processions passed, and being so narrow, you could reach out and stroke the statues, if you really wanted. It is hard to see these beloved houses belonging to people I do not know. Watching these strangers walk in and out of these houses is painful. I wish I could go back to that time long ago, so I could once again enjoy the innocence and the beauty of it.

Some of my cousins I am still quite close to, but my life has really changed. We are all very much taken up by our work, our homes, our cars, our sons and daughters, our investments. One of my cousins on my mom's side, Tony, died in May 1978 at the age of 13. He had Hodgkin's lymphoma. This was in 1978, and there was no cure. It was my first experience of death. I was two years older than him. It was the first separation. I visited him at the hospital, and he had just died. After they had prepared the body for burial, I saw him again. I could not sleep for many months because of the memory. I realized that death has no age, that death is a really cruel reality. I promised myself that I would live an intense life while I had the opportunity. We suffered a lot as a family in the following days, months, and years. The memory of the funeral is still very clear in my mind. The date of his death is the only date which I remember. I would be able to paint the color of his body at the moment of death. That was well over forty years ago.

I have seen three corpses in my lifetime. One of the children in the neighborhood once convinced us to go to the local cemetery to see the body of a man whose funeral was being held that morning at the local cemetery. I still remember this man's name. He was called Bendu. I really have no idea why we went. It is a memory that has stayed, despite the decades that have passed. The third person was my grandfather Nazzareno. My grandmother had died six months prior, and he was residing at Holy Family Home in Naxxar, which back then was still run by the Little Sisters of the Poor. In this case, I was present at the moment of death and could see my grandfather turning pale until he looked like wax.

There were a number of family traumas which I learned about through nanna Pawla. One of them was the death of her own father, who died on his own doorstep, at the address on Cross Street, where my great aunts and uncle still lived. He had fallen off a donkey-drawn cart, and died instantly. It was never made clear to me whether this great-grandfather died because he fell, or whether he fell because he died. I also remember nanna Pawla mentioning the suicide of a young woman related to us who hung herself at her parents' house some time after giving birth to a baby boy. No one knew anything about postnatal depression back then. My other great-grandfather, on my paternal side, also died a sudden death. Peter Gatt, nanna Vitor's father, fell ill and died soon after, leaving a wife and two very young girls, the eldest being only four years old. Ġużeppa, their mother, was widowed there and then. For a woman to be left with two young children at the turn of the twentieth century must have been especially hard. There were surely other difficult moments in the life of my family. Members of the family who were born with some kind of deformity, relatives who died as infants, illnesses that had to be endured, marriages that failed, natural miscarriages, and so much more. Time may bury these stories and memories may become faint, but we inherit the effects of these traumas, and we suffer along with our ancestors, even while knowing so little about their stories.

After Year 6, I went to Lily of the Valley Girls' Secondary School in Mosta. It is coed nowadays, but not at the time. I spent two years at this school. It is the school where I first started studying French. It is the school where I had home economics and learned some simple cooking. Many of my teachers from that time still recognize me today. One of them, Pauline Quattromani, was a friend of mine for many years. I have since lost touch, but I taught alongside her as a student teacher in training, and for many years I met her at guidance teachers' meetings organized by the education department. Ms. Quattromani never married. She used to teach me math, and I loved her a lot. I was not the best student in the world in terms of behavior, but I used to read a lot, and I did my homework meticulously. Once again, I remember my teachers very well. Ms. Roberts used to teach me science, Mr. Agius taught me English, Mr.

Sciberras taught me Maltese and civics. I loved Mr. Sciberras, and I used to go and meet him at the staff-room door in order to carry his stuff. Mr. Sciberras was also a poet, and I showed off a bit during his class. I received two prizes at this school: in civics and in French. Besides the teachers, I also remember a few other things: I remember my participation in the prize-day show. I was dressed like a flower, with huge petals propped with wire around my neck, and we sang "Sunrise, Sunset" from the musical *Fiddler on the Roof*. The music teacher also chose a few of us students to sing at the Manoel Theatre. We sang along with, and mimed, two war-protest songs: "Universal Soldier" and "All We Are Saying Is Give Peace a Chance." I also remember the efficiency apartment that the school had, and which we sometimes cooked in for our home economics class. I remember us cooking madeleines, rock cakes, butterfly cakes, and a shepherd's pie. It was such a good feeling to return home carrying your goodies and to share the outcome of one's cooking with the other members of the family.

At that time, we were expected to carry out corrections—that is, to rewrite sections of our work which had been incorrectly done. I remember that my English teacher once wrote "Correction" in red right across a whole page of my copybook. That made me livid. I had not done my correction from the previous essay, but he had literally ruined the whole of my copybook because of that. For someone like me, who would tear out the page if it were not sufficiently neat, that was too harsh a punishment. Forty-five years later, and I still have not forgiven him!

I used to eat a lot at this time. My sandwiches were two huge slices of Maltese bread with omelets sandwiched between them. I used to have to open my mouth very wide to get a bite. I was embarrassed by the smell of my lunch, but I loved the taste of it. Sometimes, I would eat the whole of my lunch before school had even started. It is not a good feeling knowing that you have to spend the rest of your day without any lunch because you ate it before school had even started. My mother did not give us money to spend at the school tuckshop, so I would have to stay hungry until I got home.

I was also very active at this time. There was a lot of rope-jumping, racing and elastics. The latter was a game which we played using a length of elastic that was cut and sewn to make a band, which was held by two girls at the ankles. A third player would jump inside this band, across it, on top of it, and then outside it. After each turn, the band would be moved further up the body of the two girls holding the elastic until it reached their neck. I loved this game, and I was really good at it. Many consider this jumping game to be of Chinese origin. This is really interesting. Malta was on very good terms with China at the time, through Mintoff's connections. Mr. Dom Mintoff was prime minister of Malta from 1955 till 1958 and then again between 1971 and 1984. He made a deal with China and visited China, along with Lorry Sant, in 1972, a year after being elected prime minister. And I believe that it is quite possible that this is when the game came to Malta.

There were other teachers at Lily of the Valley. Ms. Apap, who used to teach me home economics, and Mr. Abdilla were probably the most significant. Both of them were members of the Society of Christian Doctrine. I remember that I once got full marks on the home economics exam. I am not sure whether this was in Form 1 (Year 7) or in Form 2 (Year 8). But that was the only time I got a perfect grade. Mr. Abdilla was still a student, and he used to teach me French. Both subjects were very close to my heart, and I still remember the first lesson of the French textbook by heart. We had *La France en Direct* by Janine Capelle. I also have very clear memories of the school playground as it stood at the time, as well as some recollection of the bullying that went on at the school. I particularly remember two students from Naxxar who would today be set on the autism spectrum and who, it was said, had nits. One of them I still see very often, because she lives in my mother's neighborhood. How little we knew about injustice back then!

The school library was a haven. This is where I read the whole Enid Blyton series: *The Famous Five, The Secret Seven, Malory Towers,* and so on. I read incessantly. I loved fiction and would read anything with some adventure featuring in it. But I soon ran out of books to read, and this was when I started going to the national library in Beltissebh, at first with my mother, and then on my own. I believe that my reading really helped me mature, even if what I read was mostly fiction. I matured because I became an interesting conversationalist. Over time, I also met many people, some of whom had suffered a lot. Some of them shared their most intimate secrets with me and shed tears as they did so. And this made me sensitive to the suffering of others. I realized that everyone had his or her personal story to live through and pain to bear. It also made me conscious of the sacred space that is created when there is a really intimate encounter, however fleeting that may be.

What is really significant is that this was the first time that I was making friends with people from outside of Naxxar. The catchment area for my first secondary school was quite small, covering Mosta, Naxxar, and Għargħur. I still had my Naxxar friends: Mary-Anne and Henriette in particular. But now, there were others. I had friends who stayed on with me until Form 5, even when I proceeded to Form 3 (Year 9) in another school. Brigette, Florence, and Carmen, the three girls from Mosta, and Josette Debono from Naxxar, were very good friends of mine. I remember the laughter during the lessons. Sometimes I was unruly. At this time, I was already wearing the MUSEUM badge with the phrase "*Verbum Dei Caro Factum Est*," signalling my association with the Society of Christian Doctrine. Mr. Sciberras used to scold me when I was misbehaving, saying, "Imbasta bil-baġġ" (meaning "I would have expected better behavior from you, since you are wearing that badge"). I could be quite disruptive—I was very talkative, and I was always looking for a good laugh, but there was no evil in me. I always did my homework. I did not as yet know how to study, but my mother was never very demanding. None of my family members had graduated, and my parents never imposed upon us any dream of theirs.

I had what I would call a lovely childhood. I always had someone to play with at home, being one of five children. My brother Reno was excellent company. Victoria and Chris were quite a few years younger, but we played with them, too. We had a playroom at home, which actually consisted of a long and narrow space where we kept a huge wooden box for our toys. I still remember how much I hated putting the toys back into this box once I was finished with them. My parents later changed this room into a downstairs shower and toilet. I hated housework and shopping. I would rather read in bed for days on end than clean the house. And shopping seemed beyond me. I would endlessly repeat the list of items my mom had ordered, and still always forget something that I was supposed to buy. There was a village grocery store in Parish Street at that time, owned by two sisters who had never gotten married. Parish Street is now almost impossible to cross because of the traffic going through it every second of the day. But when we were children, our mother would let us go on our own.

I also had a "boyfriend" at that time: one of the boys who lived in the neighborhood, a certain Stephen. I preferred him over all the other boys in our street. I was still around ten years old, but my ability to love outside my family was already growing. This boy used to help me feel special. Sometime later, there was another boy whom I got to know at school. The primary school at the time was not yet coed. The boys' primary school was on one side, whereas the girls' primary school was on the other, with different entrances, different playgrounds, and different head teachers. This boy used to come and look for me at home after school. I believe that this boy's name was Tony. But I am not quite sure. One day, this same boy called at my grandmother's house. It was a huge embarrassment for me, because all my aunts found out that I had a boyfriend. This one was not one of the neighborhood boys, so his visit seemed a bit in excess. At one time, he gave me money for no particular reason. I remember my mother telling me that I should not accept money from boys because if I do, the boys could be expecting something in return. I do not think that I understood what my mother meant at the time. I was only ten or eleven years old! But I never forgot what my mother told me.

The school day was really long, with a long midday break and a dismissal at 3:45 p.m. But 4:00 p.m. was a great time of the day. My mother would bake doughnuts for us, and we would dip big *biskuttelli* (*biscottelli*, in Italian) or toasted bread and butter in our tea, watch the circles of oil floating in our cups, and eat the leftover pieces of *biskuttelli* with a teaspoon. There was a bakery on Main Street, just three doors down from my grandmother, and we would buy big bags of these Maltese *biskuttelli* or *krustini*. No one makes them in the same way anymore. My mother's kitchen and fridge were always full of food. My mom would buy huge boxes of ripe fruits from the fruit-and-vegetable truck, depending on the season. I remember eating ripe bananas and ripe peaches, which she bought in huge quantities from Nenu.

When I was in Year 6, I found out how sexual intercourse happens. It was a girl from our neighborhood who told me as we were walking home from school. She said that her aunt had explained everything to her. I only told my mother about this occasion some months ago. My mother would have been too embarrassed to talk about sex. She is one of those women who knew nothing about sex until she married my father, and, although she wanted children, she never got over the shock of having to go through the sexual act in order for her to conceive.

I grew up very innocent with respect to sex. In my childhood, I used to think that it was enough for a man and a woman to love each other in order for them to have a child. Nothing else was required. But even after I found out the "facts of life," my interest in sexual intimacy did not grow. My boyfriends remained just friends. There was never any touching or physical play between us. When the village feast arrived, I would go to the village playground and meet new boys. It was here that I smoked my first cigarette. Someone had given it to me. My aunt walked past the playground and saw me smoking and told my mother about it. My mother's reaction was the best anyone could wish for. She did not express any anger. She just explained to me that smoking could be addictive, and that I must be really careful not to get addicted to cigarettes. I never smoked again.

Our parish church is dedicated to Our Lady of Victories, and so our village feast was, and still is, held every September 8 What I lacked in facial features would be made up through my clothes. I was never a beauty, but my mother could sew, and at a time when buying ready-made clothes would have cost a fortune, my mother could sew me a dress, or even a suit, for a few shillings, having bought fabric by the yard from a village market or a sewing shop. My mother used *The Burda* style magazine, which included sewing patterns. I could choose the style of dress I wanted, and she would buy the material and sew it for me. I had a good figure, but I started wearing reading glasses when I was in Year 6, my hips started growing as I matured, I had lost my front teeth in a fall, and I often had an unpleasant body odor under my armpits, even though I washed. These things made me feel very inferior.

I remember a couple of things very vividly from my childhood. I remember us playing with beads and with marbles. I remember writing down the number of cars which went past our house. Not far from our house, there were a number of plots which still had nothing built on them. One of them belonged to a family popularly known as Tal-Bonu. Some time ago, it was turned into Charles and Ron Café, but when we were children, it was an abandoned field. We would use the stones to build walls and find cardboard or some other material to provide a roof for shelter and just sit and talk inside while it lasted. On one occasion, we all got food poisoning. There was a castor tree, and we thought it would be a good idea to eat the bean-like seeds inside the shell. We all survived, but we were sick for a couple of days after that. On another occasion, we were in another field across the road. There was the skeleton of a car, which we thought we would push over the edge into another field that was a story or so below it. As we were doing this, my clothes got entangled in some scrap metal, and I ended up falling alongside the car. I was lucky enough to land on my two feet, and no damage was done. But that memory of floating in the air as I came down and that perfect landing has remained with me.

On summer evenings, we would sit on our front porch, or on the porch of one of our neighbors, and just chat and play. Sometimes, we said the rosary together. At other times, we played "Pizzi Pizzi kanna," a traditional children's rhyme, which meant repeating the rhyme while counting one's fingers. The finger on which the rhyme stopped would be folded in. Whoever got all of his or her fingers folded in was declared the winner. Or else we would play "I Spy."

Soon enough, however, we grew older and no longer played outside on the streets. We had become friends who said nothing but "hello" and "goodbye" to each other. One of the neighborhood boys once told me that if I remained in the SDC, he would not talk to me again. He did not keep his word. Today, he lives in Australia, but he does talk to me when he visits.

In the summer between Forms 2 and 3, I met a boy nick-
named "the Scotch." We met during a summer camp. I had attended
summer school that year, and one of the events that was organized
was a weekend sleepover in the barracks at Għadira Bay. This was
probably one of the first times that I slept at a place not belonging
to anyone within my family. But my brother Reno was at the same
live-in camp. This boy whom I mentioned was there with another
group of teens. He was totally unsuited for me, but I really liked
him. He was fourteen years old, he was from the south, he already
drank excessively, and he had a girlfriend. I was still twelve, very
naive, and inexperienced. But we were very much fascinated by
each other. This was the first time I was kissed. But I did not really care for kissing. That year, he came to the village feast, and we
were hoping to meet. But when I reached the village playground, he
had already left the village. There were no cell phones at the time,
and, as I mentioned earlier, we did not as yet have a fixed telephone
line. My mother used to have to go to a neighbor in order to make
her important phone calls. So there were no possibilities for us two
being in touch. It is amazing how a life changes direction by something so coincidental, and how the technologies of the era have the
power to shape our lives.

In Form 3 of secondary school, I started going to Marija
Reġina, a girls' secondary school in Blata l-Bajda. It was a compre-
hensive school—that is, a public school that did not select its intake
on the basis of academic achievement or aptitude. It must have
been very challenging for the teachers at the school. It was certainly
challenging for the students. Physical fights between girls were all
a part of the norm, particularly in the playground. The thing that
really saved the school was the annual musical that was produced
and directed by Mr. Godwin Scerri and Mr. Frank Tanti. They were
amazing performances that made me fall in love with musicals.
One of the musicals which was produced for one of the prize days
during those years was *South Pacific*. Another one was *West Side
Story*. I watched the rehearsals whenever I got the opportunity, and
I learned most of the songs by heart.

I got to know girls from towns and villages outside the catchment area of the Lily of the Valley school. So, besides students from

Mosta, Naxxar, and Għargħur, in my class there were now students from St Paul's Bay, Mġarr, Mellieħa, Valletta, Marsa, Gżira, Żurrieq, and Pietà. I spent three years with these people. Two of my classmates later emigrated to Canada, one to Italy, one to the UK, and one to Australia. This helped us remain in touch, since those who returned to Malta on holidays always appreciated meeting up with the group. In fact, we have met various times over the years, and we have a Whatsapp group where we share our joys and our sorrows. All of them are married with children, except for myself. Some of them are also grandmothers. Our relationship has matured over the years. One of the people I felt closest to in class was Diane, since I sat at a desk right next to hers. But there were others: Antoinette, Victoria, and Natalie, to name a few.

At Marija Reġina Girls' Secondary School, I loved my teacher for French, Ms. Agius, as well as my teacher for English, Ms. Dalmas. There were others: Fr. John Ciarlo and Fr. Michael Zammit for religion. They were good teachers, but my favorites were always those who were not too formal and who had a sense of humor. I had opted for history and geography, which may not have been a good choice, seeing that I had never traveled and that European history was too complicated for my brain. But I loved French, and I loved English.

Some of my classmates were just amazing, especially in the way they juggled their time. Some of them already had steady boyfriends. They went out with boys, were active in church, competed in singing competitions, went to discos—which were the trend at the time—and still managed to get very good grades. I was not like that. I did not go out with boys, I did not sing in choirs, I did not go to my friends' houses for overnight stays. My friends at school used to go to discos and then sleep at each other's houses. They knew that I did not go to discos and that I did not have many friends who were boys. None of them invited me to their houses on the weekends. This used to hurt me a little. I sometimes felt a little left out, although I was aware that I would not have fit in had I been invited. Neither did I go to Valletta when a naval ship berthed, although I found sailors in uniform very attractive. I had even inquired about becoming a naval Wren around this time—that is, about serving

in the British Royal Navy. I loved the idea of travel. I was aware
that my own father had been to Australia and back before he got
married to my mother. He was only there for a few years, but I used
to fantasize about emigrating to Australia, probably having been
influenced by one of our group of friends who had grown up in
Australia and who joined us in Form 3 (Year 9).

I was an average student. I used to spend a lot of time at the
MUSEUM—until late in the evening, in fact. Sometimes we would
be cleaning the building, at other times we would be putting together concerts for the younger children, organizing the book or the
filmstrip library, rehearsing for plays, and so on and so forth. There
was no one at home to push me to study, and I am still surprised
that I passed my ordinary level examinations. I did not get a single
A. But I was qualified enough to get into Sixth Form.

From Form 3 onwards, I was already taking the SDC seriously.
I was first attracted to it because of the activities that were offered
and the initiatives that I myself was allowed to take. As early as
1976, I had already started to attend an annual three-day retreat.
I was still thirteen years old. These were really powerful events. I
still have the notes taken during those weekends. The SDC youth
leaders would generally get a young priest to talk to us about Jesus
or about the saints. Stories were told and inspirational sayings were
read out, and since I always had notebooks into which I would jot
things down, I could be reminded of them and inspired by them
over and over again.

These retreats were held at the Naxxar MUSEUM center on
Castro Street. Every summer for decades, the catechetical center
would be changed into a retreat center. Curtain partitions would be
put up, and one would construct a temporary monastic cell consisting of a bed and a bedside table, as well as a water jug and a basin to
refresh oneself with. The retreatants would provide the sheets and
the towels themselves. There was little comfort, but the food at these
retreats was good, the music was great, and the sense of collegiality
was amazing. We would keep the silence throughout, which was
hard and sometimes very funny. There we would be seated at a table
for eight people, and the very sounds of the knives and the forks
would seem so ludicrously loud that we would look at each other

and have to control our laughter. The sessions which took place on the flat roof in the evenings were always memorable. We would carry chairs onto the highest roof. There would be singing, accompanied by the guitars, and a lot of deep and personal sharing, which I loved. This created a very profound group spirit. I attended these annual retreats throughout my youth. When I became an adult, I found that the house was not really sufficient for meditating. The garden was small, there was very little privacy, the showers were too few, and there was always someone at every nook and cranny, even when you needed alone time. But the chapel was big, and the sermons were generally very good. And praying late into the night was an experience to look forward to. I loved these retreats so much that I would generally offer to help out in the kitchen at least once every summer. This is were I learned to clean the toilets, set the table, and peel the onions. I learned very little cooking there. But the camaraderie was great.

My formation within the Society was based on two principle pillars: the Scriptures and the lives of the saints. We were taught sentences from the Bible by heart, we read the the Old Testament books in narrative form from an old book that was at the center, and we had Bible studies called *Qaghdat,* which the founder of the Society and the original members of the Society had written, with lessons to be learned from each text and resolutions based on the text.

As a child, we would have weekly "lectures," as they were called. Filmstrips were the order of the day. Each SDC center had its own Elmo projector, which could project filmstrips onto a wall while a member of the Society would give a lecture—that is, describe what could be seen on the slide, narrate the story of that filmstrip, or explain the subject following the small booklet which came with the filmstrip and which had explanations for each and every slide. Most of these filmstrips where produced by the Italian publishing house Elledici (LDC) and were in Italian, requiring translation for the non-Italian-speaking members of the Society. I myself made many such translations when I was in my late teens. Having learned some Italian from the TV channels that we were exposed to, I could translate these small booklets, although I had to have an Italian dictionary throughout the translation, so as not to mistranslate.

The saint who was especially significant to me at the time was Saint John Bosco. The center owned various filmstrips ranging from John Bosco's childhood and youth to his experience as a founder of the international Salesian community. We also had filmstrips of Dominic Savio and Michele Magone, two of the boys at John Bosco's oratory who became saints at a young age. John Bosco became my hero. His talents, his joie de vivre, his vivaciousness were very attractive to me. I looked upon him as an example for me in my own journey and as a model for a future within the Society of working with children and young people. That is, if I decided to stay. But the possibility had already occurred to me.

There were other saintly figures that stood out in my formation—Maria Goretti and Gemma Galgani were presented to us as models of saintliness. There were various other saints whose lives we would commemorate every year, but these were the most influential in my case. Then there were also the Bambo filmstrips, which everyone loved. Bambo was an African boy in some missionary land. I remember very little about his adventures, but the filmstrips were meant to acquaint us with the work of missionaries working abroad, as well as provide us with a model of goodness, which Bambo always was.

I was also very much influenced by books written by American Christian evangelists, such as David Wilkerson's *The Cross and the Switchblade* and Nicky Cruz's *Run Baby Run*. These books filled me with enthusiasm for Christ, for evangelization, and for working with young people. Although I have been an evangelist and a catechist my entire life, I never really could communicate well with tough, streetwise young people. Still, I received a lot of inspiration from these books. Kenneth Roberts's *Playboy to Priest* was also very inspiring as I was growing up and helped me in my choice of vocation. Later on, I would read all of John Powell's books. Powell wrote many books dealing with psychology and Catholic theology which were very popular among the members of the Society during that time and were an important part of our formation. Later on came Thomas Merton's *The Seven Storey Mountain* and Corrie ten Boom's

The Hiding Place. What a gem it was to have access to these books. The Catholic bookshop run by the Male Section of the Society of Christian Doctrine, Preca Library, was full of such gems, each one of which acted as a stone in the building of my spirituality.

I became a full member of the Society in June 1982, the same year in which I started my BEd (Hons) at the University of Malta. This is why I never got married. Celibacy is required for all full members of the Society. The Society was still very much a traditional one when I first joined. Members were required to dress in black, to not wear jewelery or makeup, and to not pursue the changing fashions of the time. I started wearing the black dress when I was thirteen, five years before I became a full member. I was not alone. There were various fourteen- to seventeen-year-old young ladies from other towns and villages who were going through the same process. We would meet in Floriana on Saturdays, where Mary Chircop and others would organize talks for us. Some of these talks were life changing. I clearly remember listening enthusiastically to Patri Guido Schembri, a member of the Order of Friars Minor (1923–2012). Patri Guido had pursued studies in Holy Scripture at the Pontifical Biblical Institute in Rome. His talks on the Jewish and Christian scriptures were truly compelling.

I met some great people within the Society. Some of them later left the Society. There was Anna Mangion, Amalia Giuliano, Doris Borg, Stephanie Bezzina, Marlene Polidano, Cettina Galea, and so many others over the span of thirty years. These were people with whom I shared a lot of fun times, as well as my formation and prayer. Our three-day stays in Gozo every year where amazing. It was pure joy. Mary Chircop and Phyllis Falzon were others who were especially significant at this time. I have memories of the vans packed by over-excited young women being driven by the members Carmen Farrugia and Franca Buttigieg. There were no laws back then concerning safety belts, and being shot out of your seat whenever the van driver pressed the brake pedal was considered to be part of the fun. Having to vacate the van and walk so that the tired van would be able to climb the steep hill in Gozo at Daħlet Qorrot was at the time a laughable matter. We spent late summer evenings at public playgrounds. Singing at the top of our voices songs that

Franca had created was considered very funny. We had these sleep-overs in Għajnsielem, where there is a disability center today, just up the hill from Mġarr Harbour.

There were also members of the SDC who died young. Mary Demicoli was a case in point. She was one of the unforgettable comedians within the Society. Unfortunately, she lost her battle with stomach cancer when she was still in her thirties. Years later, we also lost Anna Camilleri, who died of cystic fibrosis, and Joyce Mintoff. All of these members had one thing in common: a sense of humor. Each of them was admirable in her own way. Then there was Donia Baldacchino, the Maltese professor of nursing who died in 2017 of lung cancer. Donia's passing away affected the Society immensely, since she had held various administrative positions within the Society.

But perhaps the most amazing woman I met within the Society was Marija Xuereb. She was the superior at the Naxxar catechetical center for most of my years there. She was an amazing listener, and she felt comfortable with sharing things with me as well, although she was older than me. We would sometimes spend hours sitting and talking on a bench in the hallway of the Naxxar SDC center after all the others had left. This was a time when the number of members at the center was still significant. There must have been around twenty or twenty-five adult full members working at the center. Marija and I would talk about everything, but especially about God and about the MUSEUM. She did not work outside the home, but she was a seamstress. She sewed sofa and armchair covers for her clients. She had one brother who was a Jesuit and another brother who was a Diocesan priest, who became the archpriest of Naxxar at one point. Marija and I were related. Her mother and my paternal grandmother were sisters. I have already mentioned them. The two siblings: Angela (Marija's mother) and Vitor (my dad's mother) lost their father when they were under the age of four. Marija often shared with me one of her disappointments in life: not having been given an education. She was a girl, and she lived at a time when education was for boys; girls used to be withdrawn from school to help with the housework or in the fields.

One of the most frightening experiences in my life involved Marija. It was a really stormy night. Marija, myself, and various other members had been cleaning the center: dusting the furniture, cleaning the window panes, and washing the floors. There was an electricity cut right in the middle of all this activity. Whenever that happened, even the water supply in the water faucets would stop. There was one particular faucet which we had in the restrooms and which we used to fill our buckets for washing the floor. We left the center intending to continue with the cleaning the following day. I went home, had my supper, changed into my pajamas, and went to bed. Suddenly—it must have been around 11:00 p.m.—I thought of the faucet. I realized that the faucet may not have been closed, and that with the return of the electricity supply, the water could flood the place. I decided to get out of bed, put a coat on, and leave the house, despite the rain, the lightning, the thunder, and the late hour. I walked toward Castro Street and toward the center. The streets were dark and deserted, but I could see a figure coming toward me. I realized that it was Marija Xuereb, wearing a coat over her pajamas. It transpired that she, too, had been lying in bed, had thought of the faucet, and, fearing a flooding, had decided to get out of bed, put a coat over her nightdress, and leave the house, despite the weather and the late hour. I was profoundly shocked. It felt like a paranormal experience to me. Had we become so close that the same thought would come to us at the same time, and that we would make the same decision and meet a few steps from the door? My reaction that night was fear.

Some years later, when Marija was no longer stationed at the Naxxar center, she was diagnosed with motor neurone disease. I remember her calling me on the fixed line to tell me about it. How little I understood back then what a shock the diagnosis would have been for her! It had started with her finding it difficult to speak because her tongue muscle would not obey her commands. Slowly, she got worse, until, toward the end, she was completely debilitated. I remember her coming to the Naxxar center and telling me how she would have loved to live the rest of her life surrounded by children, but how she could no longer be understood by them. She could no longer catechize. Toward the end, she could no longer speak, although she could write legibly, even if shakily. She was only sixty when she passed away. This was on November 15, 1998. I cried heartily at her funeral. She was truly one of my greatest benefactors and truest friends, although she was twenty-five years my senior.

I remember many members of the Society from my childhood and youth. Most significant among these was Vincenza Azzopardi, also from Naxxar. Vincenza acted as the assistant to the superior general for many years. Is-Superjura Ċensa, as she was known, was an important figure within the Society. She was responsible for turning the Naxxar center into a full-blown retreat center during the summer. I remember her talking on the phone for hours, on the fixed line—that is, organizing events; I remember the traditional Maltese trifle (like a gateau with custard) which she used to make for the retreatants; I remember her dignified posture. She was quite strict as a superior. I remember her calling me to the side and correcting me for having been whistling a tune. I did not take it kindly. In my opinion at the time, she had some very strange, old-fashioned, oppressive opinions that I did not care for much. I appreciated kindness, and, in my mind, she represented austerity rather than kindness. But I never doubted her goodwill, her commitment, her hard work, and her dedication to the Society. She spent the last years of her life at the Little Sisters of the Poor in Naxxar. Vincenza died on May 6, 2006, at the age of ninety-three.

During the time of my formation, there was just one person who was receiving the same formation alongside myself: Rita Catania. At the time, the members still wore black. It was not exactly a habit, as in the case of nuns, but it was a kind of uniform. Members had been wearing it since the beginning of the Society. Rita and I started wearing this black uniform when we were thirteen years old. At first, we would wear the black dress at meetings, as was the custom within the Society at the time. All I can say is that I was very embarassed, and I did not want my school friends to see me with the members of the MUSEUM, although when they did see me, they told me that the black dress really suited me.

It was only when I was in Form 5 that I started to learn some independence. I was otherwise very fearful. By the age of eleven, I was already attending a school that was outside my village, but transport was provided, and it was a private bus which I took. Using public transport was a huge challenge for me. Although my father had a car, he never drove us anywhere. My father had learned how to drive when he was around thirty years old, and he never felt confident driving in the central areas. He used the car to drive to our fields, which were just down the hill from Naxxar, going toward Salina. I guess that was a godsend, however tough for me at the time. I started going everywhere on my own.

I started Sixth Form in October of 1979, and I did my first year of Sixth Form at the Old University building in Valletta. The second year was held at the Polythechnic in Imsida. Here, I really started taking my studies seriously. At home, I was clashing a lot with my parents, my brothers, and my sister. We were a family of seven, and the house was crowded. With one television in the home, there was no shortage of arguments. I started sleeping on my own in the room which we had on the roof. It was a room used for storage, full of stuff that had been set aside: old frames, old pieces of furniture, and an old table. The access to it was through a roofed terrace on the second floor, and since three of the walls of this room were exterior walls and its floor was a cement floor, it could get very cold, but I had the privacy which I longed for. And I could wake up and read at night if I wanted.

We lost a lot of time when I was at Sixth Form, since we had to change the premises from Valletta to the Polytechnic building in Msida, which currently houses the Ġ. F. Abela Junior College. There was a lot of disorganization while the move was taking place. Not only was there this move from Valletta to Msida, but our course was suddenly reduced from three years to two. It was the Labour Party which was in government at the time, and there was a lot of political turmoil, particularly within the field of education. The government was convinced that work experience was essential, and it set up the pupil-worker scheme for pupils within the Sixth Form, for university students, and for those attending the Technical Institute. The pupils at the Sixth Form were totally unprepared for this. Meetings with Dr. Philip Muscat, the minister of education at the time, turned into rowdy demonstrations and protests. Dr. Muscat was the minister of education between 1981 and 1983. I myself worked at Menrad, the eyewear factory in San Gwann.

Being a machine operator was tough for me. I never managed to achieve much in terms of production. I woke up at 5:00 a.m. every morning, went to 5:30 a.m. mass, and was at work at 7:00 a.m. It was hard. During the second-year work phase, which lasted seven months, I worked in the factory office, which was easier. I was not alone. There were at least three other students: Natalie Abela, who later joined the Sisters of Charity and with whom I have kept in touch throughout the years, and two more girls, Maria Micallef and Antoinette Cachia. Many students dropped out that year. We were expected to go for tutorials on Saturday mornings, but that was also hard. After working hours, it was difficult to find the energy to write essays in Maltese, English, or French, which where the subjects I had taken, and after a week at the factory, it was difficult to take the bus to school on Saturday mornings and find out that you were the only one who had turned up, so your lecturer was focused on just you during that tutorial. I guess I should count myself lucky that I got all this personal attention, but it did not seem to be the case at the time. In spite of everything, I did really well in my advanced levels. Besides the exams in Maltese, English, and French, I also sat for the exam in religion, and I got an A in that. The formation I had received at SDC was sufficient for that.

A lot was going on in my life around this time. I bought my first guitar and started playing it. I never went for lessons. My sister was being taught how to play it at her primary school, and I learned what she knew. My sister and I would spend a lot of time at home playing the guitar and singing church hymns. My sister played with a group every Sunday. This was at the Jesuit Chapel in Naxxar, dedicated to Our Lady of the Way, the same one where my mother had had her spiritual experience. Also living within this Jesuit community was one Jesuit priest who helped me immensely. His name was Fr. Charles Delia, SJ. He was always available for me. There were no time limits, and we used to discuss my studies as well as my spiritual challenges and the issue of my vocation, about which I had started thinking with some seriousness. I still feel very much obliged to him because he saw me holistically. I sought his help until I was around twenty years old—that is, for close to eight years. It was very hard for me to find another spiritual director after he had traveled to Rome.

I was already wearing the black dress daily when I started Sixth Form, and this used to distinguish me from the rest. I could not integrate with the others. I was always sticking out. In class, the lecturers used to throw at me the most controversial questions about the Bible or about theology. I felt that I knew very little, and I used to be embarrassed. But when I was about to choose the main subject at university, I could not pursue theology. In Malta, we only had one university, and the faculty of theology had been transferred to the seminary. I chose education instead, with English as the main subject, and I never regretted this decision. The course which led to the BEd (Hons) was five years long. They were difficult years, but beautiful at the same time. I made friends with some great people— people who were intellectual and very profound, and who were not happy with superficial answers. People who challenged my way of thinking with their philosophy. The ones I found most difficult to accept were not the communists or those who were openly anti-clerical but rather those who were overambitious academically and who would snatch the library books even before the reading list was published. We argued, fought, competed aggressively, laughed, and cried. We called our group the BEd Cuties. But we could be fierce and insubordinate.

I believe that five years was too long a course for a profes-sional degree in teaching. But students were expected to teach for six months and study for the other six months, so there would have been little time for the more academic aspect of the degree had the course been shorter. The lecturers at the time, who included people like Professor Peter Vassallo, whom I admired immensely, were clearly frustrated at having to reduce their courses, which they had previously given to BA students, to the time now allocated for the BEd (Hons). But it was a great course. The units covering literature were particularly interesting, especially those on medieval litera-ture, on Commonwealth literature, and on the modern novel. And then there was always Shakespeare! The tragedies, the comedies, and the histories were all enriching in their own right. I loved these lectures. I did not enjoy the subsidiary subject so much. We had been forced to choose primary and middle education as a subsidiary, in order that it would make it easier to find a job. We would thus be qualified to teach both at the secondary and at the primary levels.

As previously mentioned, the years I was at university were, politically, very turbulent. In 1983, Archbishop Mercieca faced threats by the government, led by the then Labour Party prime minister, Dom Mintoff, of seizing most of the church's property. The year 1984 was the year when there was the church school issue and the teachers' strike. Church schools were first impeded from raising their fees to cover their growing expenses. A nine-week strike, ordered by the Malta Union of Teachers in 1984, was the climax of an industrial dispute that went on for years. The battle cry was "*Jew b'xejn jew xejr*" (meaning "Either free of charge or nothing"). At the time, church schools were viewed as elitist and as a form of social segregation, and, in its electoral manifesto for the 1981 election, the Labour Party had promised free schools for everyone. It was only the stiff resistance of the parents at the time that finally made the Labour Party give in.

There were thirteen students in the English group, only one of whom was not Maltese. He was Bulgarian, and his name was Vladimir Phillipov. Two students from this group where directly involved in leading the University Students' Council (KSU) at this time of crisis. I myself went to most of the meetings organized by the KSU, as well as those organized by the Malta Movement of Teachers. We demonstrated at the university, shouting antigovernment slogans. We were at the university when the Labour Party thugs came. We were in Floriana—at a friend's house—when the archbishop's curia was attacked by shipyard workers who entered the premises and damaged paintings and broke glass, furniture, and statues. This was in September 1984. According to Sammy Meilaq, a former Dom Mintoff aide, the 1984 attack on the archbishop's curia in Floriana by a number of shipyard workers "was of benefit to the faith in Malta."[2] Well, all I can say is that I was traumatized by it.

The anticlericalism was very strong. This was the time when I would be on a bus and people would start offending me from the other side for no other reason except that I was wearing the black uniform of SDC, so I was identified with the church. I remember one such instance. If I remember correctly, this was the same day as the attack on the curia. Someone got onto the bus while swearing and shouting offensively against the archbishop of the time: Guzeppi Mercieca. I had been through too much on that day. I could no longer take it. I started sobbing and shaking. I must have shocked the man sitting next to me on the bus. After a while, this same man took my hand and held it until I stopped sobbing. I do not know who the man was, but he had been sensitive enough to realise that I needed consolation. I am obliged to him even now, around forty years later.

Most of us students were antisocialist in terms of politics, and we were always uncomfortable with having figures from the Labour Party government visiting us at university. At one point, we were expecting Agatha Barbara to visit. Agatha Barbara was president of the Republic between 1982 and 1987. That was the time of the "Ġakketta Blu," or the Nationalist Party's Blue Jacket Brigade. The other students all agreed that they would come to university dressed in blue, as a symbol of resistance. I could not do that because of my uniform, so my mother sewed a blue handkerchief for me, which I used profusely during Agatha Barbara's visit to our class. Agatha Barbara was a huge joke to me back then. I have since learned to respect her. She contested the first general elections held on the granting of the new constitution in 1947, became the first woman ever to be elected to the Maltese parliament, contested all subsequent parliamentary elections, and held a seat in the House of Representatives till the day she was elected president of the Republic.

I spent most of my life within the field of education, whether as a student, as a teacher, or as a university lecturer. I remember many of the ministers of education, some of them quite clearly: Dr. Antonio Paris, Dr. Paolo Borg Olivier, Agatha Barbara, Dr. Guze Cassar, Dr. Philip Muscat, Karmenu Mifsud Bonnici, Dr. Ugo Mifsud Bonnici, Dr. Evarist Bartolo, Dr. Louis Galea, Dolores Cristina, and Dr. Justyne Caruana. Agatha Barbara was minister of education and culture between 1971 and 1976, and Mifsud Bonnici was minister of education and communications between September

1983 and May 1987. In Malta, ministers of education are often quite vocal. They are often on the eight o'clock evening news, and they are also very much physically present in schools: on prize days, graduations, school visits. Each one has his or her vision of education and a direction he or she wishes education to take. But in my experience, few of them made their project coherent or succeeded in selling their vision to the electorate.

So, how does one judge the achievement of each of them? What is it that counts? Does one judge them on the number of new schools which they built or which they refurbished? Does one judge them by the skills and talents for citizenship and employability that they provided? Does one judge them by their ability to develop the personal and social potential of children? Or by their success in helping children acquire the appropriate knowledge, key skills, competences, and attitudes? Does one judge them by their ability to provide a value-oriented formation that includes values such as equity, social justice, diversity, and inclusivity? Does one judge them by the equal opportunities they provided where quality education is concerned? Or by whether they managed to provide young people with the lifelong skills, values, and self-reliance to be independent? Or by whether they offered a wide variety of higher education and training opportunities to enable everyone to get ahead in life and develop themselves professionally? And finally, does one judge them based on the policies on education and employment which they formulated and implemented, on the legal framework that they created, or on their ability to work closely with stakeholders in the field? Clearly, not only is it difficult to judge a life, it is also difficult to judge an office.

In my early twenties, my crisis within the MUSEUM was only just beginning. I had such high hopes as to what I could achieve. I had a vision for myself within this Society. I thought I would do so much for young people. I would give all of my love, and they would love me in return. I would organize events and activities for and with young people: prayer meetings, adventure outings, treasure hunts, Bible study sessions, hikes, a good library, live-in camps, and so on. And there would be nothing but love for me from the members of the community, because I would always do my best.

Unfortunately, this utopia did not last. More often than not, the Society gave me nothing but agony. Very often, my life within the MUSEUM was a continuous denial and sacrifice—an obedient offering without any sense. I often felt that I had had enough. It was not sex which was calling me to give up everything but the thirst for freedom, the longing for some culture. I dreaded the end of the BEd course, fearing that my brain would stop thinking once I no longer had the intellectual stimulation that I encountered at university. The intellectual and cultural aspects were practically absent at the SDC center I used to attend. No one I knew had even the ordinary-level standard of education. The MUSEUM used to satisfy certain needs, but not the need for culture and critical thinking.

I did not study as much as I should have done, because I remained fully committed within the SDC. But I did not like what I was seeing. There were very few friends my age within the Society, and these I saw only on Saturdays and for a few days over the summer. Otherwise, I lived with people who were much older than me. Some of them did love me and accept me, while others were critical of whatever I did or said. Fr. Charles Delia, SJ, helped me a lot to prepare myself for when I left university so that I would be able to find a balance between my ideals and the practical life.

The friends I had were often transitory: I would make friends with peope who were studying or working with me, but I would then not keep in touch over time. I would not call or seek to meet with them. But having friends within the SDC has never been easy, either. We may be part of one society, but in general, we do not meet on a social basis, and we rarely get to know each other on an intimate level. Despite all this, people like Pauline Grech, Gaetana Saliba, Nicholina Micallef and Esther Farrugia have been a constant support. Other friends who have sustained me over the years are Abel Giglio, Fr. Joe Inguanez, Fr. Louis Caruana and Natalino Camilleri. More recently, Graziella Buttigieg has acted as my companion in adventure and my nurse. But perhaps most worthy of mention is my dear mother. My mother does not know everything about me, but she knows enough, and she accepts me totally. I love her company. She is wise, and she takes an interest in and can talk about practically everything: whether it is carpentry, gardening, sewing, house construction, cooking. She took up new hobbies in her old age: pottery in her fifties, and lace-making at the age of sixty. And she is a good conversationalist.

Victoria, my only sister, was six years younger than me, but she was always mature for her age. I could talk to her as if she were my equal, even when she was really very young. She was always as pretty as a doll, with straight hair that was never dishevelled. She could read the newspaper before she started primary school. When she was a young girl, I used to talk to her as if she were my age, and she would always understand. We would compare her to the Italian singer, dancer, and TV presenter Raffaella Carrà. Like Raffaella, my sister had a bob haircut and her hair would always return to its place when she stopped moving. In our teenage years and early adulthood, the age gap between us was more noticeable. She often jokes that the bedroom which we shared was full of stark contrasts. One half was decorated with holy pictures, and the other with hard rock images. I hated the phase when she was into hard rock. Listening to Ozzie Osbourne or Led Zeppelin was not pleasant at all, especially at a time when I listened to Simon and Garfunkel's "Like a Bridge Over Troubled Water" and "The Sound of Silence." Actually, my taste in music has varied over time, although I tend to enjoy ballads in particular. Today, my sister and I support each other a lot. I love her children and her grandson, Kane.

When I was young, the radio was all we had. I loved songs like Gerry Marsden and the Pacemakers' "You'll Never Walk Alone" from 1945, "House of the Rising Sun" by the Animals from 1964, Mary Hopkin's "Those were the Days" from 1968, Elvis Presley's "In the Ghetto" from 1969, Terry Jacks's "Seasons in the Sun," the Carpenters' "Yesterday Once More," and Tony Orlando's "Tie a Yellow Ribbon Round the Ole Oak Tree" from 1973. But I have had so many favorite songs over time. These were all songs that inspired me in some way or another, helped me appreciate life, or even got me thinking about death. Later on, there was Paul McCartney and the Wings' "Mull of Kintyre" from 1978.

The feeling that I did not fit in anywhere was a feeling that I often had to deal with. I often felt like a misfit. Sometimes I was too old, at others I was too young. Sometimes I was considered too plain, at others too attractive. Sometimes I was a misfit because of the low social class of my family of origin. At others, I was a misfit because of my tertiary education. Most of my powerful spiritual experiences have been experiences where I felt loved and accepted, where I was virtually hugged, where I felt at one with God and others. But, for years, I carried with me a deep loneliness.

I blame this also on me being so outspoken. I can be honest and earnest. I generally tell people how I feel or think, even when I know that such expressions will cause some discomfort to the other person or people. On principle, I do not believe in tact or in political correctness. My conviction is that one can only build on sincerity. According to me, acknowledging the situation and any limitations pertaining to it is the first step to ensuring change or improvement. Unfortunately, my contribution often takes the form of an outburst. What to me seems like a descriptive exercise often appears like a judgmental one for those present. Those around me are often unable to face the situation as I describe it, or else are too uncomfortable to bear it. Someone or other is often offended when I merely desire to state the facts. I have come to realize that individuals within the higher echelons of society or within institutions, and especially those who defend them blindly, are rarely open to criticism or to new ideas. Some people have claimed that I am unpolished. But these have often been men with some old-fashioned, set ideas about female behavior.

Remember that I am also a person coming from what was then a small village and belonging to the lower class, with grandparents who could not read and write, from a family of bird hunters. Yes, on my father's side, I come from a family of bird hunters, probably the most despised people on the island of Malta. Where I come from, bird hunters are considered to be equivalent to terrorists. They are land-grabbers. They are, according to some, a pressure group that exploits the political parties with threats. I rarely tell anyone about my family's pastime. People often respond with some shock when I say that my dad and brothers are hunters, so I rarely mention it. But when I hear members of the public criminalizing the hunters, it makes me sick. I find that people over-romanticize birds. Birds fly, they sing, and they may have colorful feathers, which makes them beautiful. But they can also become pests. Hunting is a primitive need, and it should only be condemned in the case of species that are at risk. But it does not make sense to prohibit hunting while allowing pesticides or fertilizers to kill the species. So, a campaign that is all for our feathered friends must be wholistic. To speak as if the hunters in Malta are the ones responsible for the scarcity of birds, and to criminalize hunters, is so simplistic.

Having lived within a family where birds and hunting were the main interest of the men, I have come to believe that hunting is not merely a bloodthirsty exercise, although I cannot deny that this can be part of it as well. The men within my family seek nature and find peace in it much more than I ever did. For years, I did not even know where the fields which we inherited from our ancestors were located. My brothers did know. They woke up at 5:00 a.m. and were there until darkness fell during most seasons. They grew crops in our fields and trapped birds. They kept pointer dogs, training them for years. It was a whole lifestyle. What they wore, what time they woke up, how they smelled upon their return from the fields, which breed of dog they chose to own, who their friends were, what books they bought, which bar they frequented at the village square, how they spent their money, how the house was decorated, and so on and so forth. It was a lifestyle that had been inherited from our ancestors. A lifestyle that many who campaign for the protection of birds have no idea about.

Despite the close proximity to this lifestyle, I never felt a part of it. The conversations at home were often centered on the birds that my brothers or their acquaintances had seen, chased, or caught, and yet I never really learned much about birds—about the types, the shapes, the colors, or the migration cycles. I did eat turtledoves and quail when they were cooked. And I did admire the art of the taxidermist when I looked at the stuffed birds in our wall unit— again, something that will shock some readers.

Of course, these could not have been the actual reasons for my ever-reappearing loneliness. My preference for reading rather than for socializing, as well as the fact that I belonged to a society that valued meditation and contemplation and emphasized the importance of spending time with God away from the hustle and bustle of life, were also causes for my solitude.

When I left university, I became a *prefetta* within the Society, which is what the Society traditionally calls the youth ministers responsible for preadolescents and adolescents. These were girls who stayed on for catechetical formation after they had received the sacrament of confirmation. The first group I was responsible for did not persevere, and I was entrusted with another group. I got to know this group very well, because they stayed on for five to seven years after their confirmation. I loved these young girls, and we formed a bond that has lasted a lifetime. Unfortunately, I did not find the right balance between ministry and self-care. My contact with adults decreased significantly, and I was spending all my time with these young people. At work, I was a teacher of English and religion, whereas at the SDC, I was once again all-absorbed by the needs of these young people. I used to, as the Maltese would say, "*niekol u norqod magħhom,*" meaning that most of my waking hours were spent in their company. We often went for takeout or to the Macdonald's and had overnight outings, so we did eat and sleep together, in a sense.

Unfortunately, despite constantly being in the company of these young people, I felt very much alone. I confessed my feelings to the other members and to my superiors within the Society, but they did not understand or support me. I was surrounded by young people, but I felt isolated. I have come up with two explanations for this. The first is that at least one of the young people did not know how to keep boundaries. She would be on the phone with me after I got home, after already having spent three or four hours together. At times, this same individual stalked me. There was another reason. In being the mentor of these beautiful, talented young people, I was completely forgotten. I felt that I was only seen as their leader and not as an individual in my own right. Being invisible felt like too much of a loss for me.

Later on, when this group of young people left, I was given another role within the Society. However, this experience had been so difficult that for many years, I was afraid of unconditional giving. I was not ready to once again go through the loss of the whole of my identity. I was willing to work hard, yes, and to give what I could, but I did not wish to lose myself so completely—that is, to deny myself everything. I still do not know whether it is possible to find a balance between the gift of self and self-fulfilment. Serving the poor is beautiful. To give oneself to people who can give you nothing in return is a generous act. But experience proved that I was not capable of it. There was a point when I had to say, "That's enough!" in order to protect myself.

When I was a child, I was on very good terms with my brother Reno, who was less than two years my junior. We never argued except for one time when, according to his narrative, he refused to obey my instructions. We argued, and he bit my hand. I do not remember this argument, but he still remembers it clearly. On the contrary, when we were children, I never agreed on anything where Francis, my elder brother, was concerned. I used to feel that my mother favored him and that she did not treat my younger brother and myself in the same way. My mother and I have, since then, often spoken about this. She insists that she never favored any one of us over the other. She explains that at that particular stage in time, my dad was returning from his work in Libya, and mom was having to adjust to having a husband at home, as well as to us kids.

Between September 1986 and June 1988, I taught at Naxxar Primary School. During these two years, I got the opportunity to see the school I was in as a child, this time as a teacher. The head of the school was Victor Fenech when I taught there. A gentlemanly figure and a well-established poet. I do not remember much about my time there, except that I spent a lot of time creating resources. And I am very proud to say that I have been a colleague to two brilliant scholars whom I knew as five-year-olds: Dr. Emanuel Buttigieg and Rev. Dr. Kevin Schembri.

The school has always remained in my life. It is where I vote during elections, it is where friends of mine still teach, and it is where many children and young people I meet at the SDC still go. The two years I taught there were beautiful and serene years. I used to teach Year 1, and I learned a lot during these years. I learned simplicity and patience. I learned how to speak softly and gently, rather than loudly and nervously. I learned to appreciate the intelligence and depth of children.

Still, I knew that I had to move. I was afraid that if I stayed at the local primary school for the rest of my life, I would end up simpleminded. My vision of what I wanted to be was much more complex than that. Teaching at a school two minutes away from my home would not suffice. I had a wider vision. I wanted a new challenge; I wanted to risk more. I applied for a transfer to a secondary school.

In September of 1988, I started teaching religion at the Junior Lyceum for Girls at St Patrick's, better known as Sir Adrian Dingli Girls' Junior Lyceum. This was situated in Pembroke. It would take me thirty minutes along a country road to get there every morning. The distance was not long, but I often had to reverse to make way for oncoming traffic. In all, I taught there for nine years. The school had once been a hospital and was not well-suited to be a school, but there were beautiful views of the sea from most of the classrooms, and that was a real consolation.

I only had an advanced level in religious knowledge at that time, but that very year I started an evening course which would lead to a bachelor's degree in Religious studies. It was a five-year course. For another five years, I spent all my free time with books. I used to enjoy the lectures, but the exams were really tiring. In the meantime, I also started teaching English, since that had been my main subject for the bachelor's degree in education. I also applied to serve as a guidance teacher at the same school. The role of the guidance teacher included counseling, career guidance, safeguarding the students, teaching our students life skills, organizing trips to places of work, carrying out research to trace the careers of ex-students of the school, and so much more. As a guidance teacher, I had many touching and rewarding experiences, but also others that were so emotionally draining that they made me wonder whether this role was something I wished to pursue for the rest of my working life.

The staff at Sir Adrian Dingli was young and sometimes quite mischievous, but it was really fun to spend one's breaks with one's colleagues. School events, like the annual Sports Day, were generally a pleasure because of the youthful spirit among the staff. One strong memory I have is that of the Eucharistic Day. This was a huge event for the school. It was always held in June close to Corpus Christi, when the weather had gotten warmer. We would prepare five rooms for adoration, one room for each one of the years. On Eucharistic Day, we would have a school mass in the school ground, and then each class would be invited to visit one of the prayer rooms for a period of organized prayer. The prayer rooms were always beautifully decorated. Members of staff would actually compete between themselves, each team attempting to create the most extraordinary sacred space. It was a lot of work, but it was a real joy. The enthusiasm of the teachers, their generosity, and their sense of competition all served to make that day a memorable one for both staff and students.

Our relationship with the head of this school was not always good. Heads of school who lock themselves in the office are never appreciated by their staff. On the other hand, overcontrolling head teachers also make it very difficult for the teachers. I experienced both while I was at this school. As a guidance teacher, I had to respond to some very urgent and complicated cases. Whether it was because a student had a mother with an addiction problem at home, or because the student was being sexually abused by a close relative, or because the relationship between the student and her parents was failing, or because students were having problems with their studies, each case took its toll on my head and my heart. I learned a lot and I grew a lot at this time. But I burned out quite quickly. I was a guidance teacher during seven of the nine years which I spent at this school, and when I applied for a transfer, I was certain that I did not wish to pursue the guidance route—that is, to continue being a guidance teacher.

On May 12, 1985, my brother Francis married Deanna, née Neil, from Kent in the UK. He emigrated to the UK in the late eighties. They had four sons: Nathan, Callum, Reece, and Kaine, who at the time of writing are fully grown men. Victoria married Aldo and had two children: Lydon and Yasmine, who are currently in their twenties. My sister and I meet or speak over the phone almost every day. My brother Reno married Tanya, née Mizzi, another beautiful woman, in the year 2000, and they have a daughter and a son: Victoria Marie and David. My younger brother, Christopher, found love in Maureen, a wonderful woman who was widowed quite young and who had Liona and Luke. Our entire lives have been a search for love, as it generally is with the whole of humanity. We seek love, and we offer it, always under the gaze of God.

I did my first course on the Enneagram with Fr. Alfred Darmanin, SJ, in 1994, or around that time. The Enneagram is a system which recognizes and describes nine personality types and allows you to identify yourself with one of these types. Once you have done that, you learn about your beliefs, your deepest motivations, your fears, and your reasons for reacting the way you do. For those of my readers who are familiar with this personality test, I am a number eight. I also followed another course called "The Enneagram and Spirituality." For a few years, I read extensively on the subject, and I became quite familiar with the character types and could identify the qualities associated with each one. Over the years, I have worked very hard to improve my personality and my character. For many years, I had to struggle to control my anger and to make physical work second nature to me. I have done all sorts of things: I attended seminars and annual three-day preaching retreats, wrote down reflections and resolutions, attended courses about character improvement and personality development, read various self-help books, went to spiritual direction, psychotherapy, and counseling, and was friends with people who were taking their prayer life seriously and who were putting their beliefs into practice. And I made sure I read and listened to inspiring stories and speeches.

My heroes have been Maximilian Kolbe, Dietrich Bonhoeffer, Martin Luther King, C. S. Lewis, Audrey Hepburn, Nelson Mandela, Christopher Reeve, Nick Vujicic, Meryl Streep, and Brené Brown, along with Abel Giglio, Annabelle Vassallo, Bjorn Formosa, Samuel Farrugia, and Arthur Vella. Each one of these has inspired me to be stronger, more resilient, more forgiving, more motivated, and also more accepting of vulnerability.

I have changed a lot over time. When I was a little girl, I was very reserved. I grew in confidence as I matured in age. Although I still suffer from anxiety, particularly when I feel overwhelmed by work or very tired, at least I now understand much better what is going on within myself and can therefore manage it better, though never completely. In general, I have learned to express my anxiety and my anger in a healthier manner.

My life has always been surrounded by books, and I have loved them. I still remember reading Charles Dickens's *Great Expectations* on the roof of our family home and crying my eyes out. Libraries, however humble, are able to give me the same sense of grandeur and solemnity as the most beautiful cathedrals. I feel that I need to be continually stimulated intellectually. I always felt that I knew very little, and I lusted for knowledge. I did two five-year-long bachelor's degrees, one in education (1982–87) and another in theology (1988–1993). This has been possible because I was always willing to sacrifice my free time to the search for wisdom and knowledge and the ecstacy provided by books. I always wanted to be an eternal student, and I feel that I have succeeded in that. The internet, with its immensely vast sources of knowledge, makes this possible to whosoever wishes to keep on learning. Virtue and wisdom are admirable and a worthy treasure to invest in, but they are not worthy of worship in themselves.

At home, I hardly helped with the housework and I never cooked, and my mother always supported my apostolate. She would make cakes for me, sew things which we needed at the catechetical center, and so on. My mother never worked outside the house, although she did do a lot of voluntary work in the parish and she sometimes sewed clothes for friends and neighbors. She was our cook, our housewife, our receptionist, our counselor. She was the one who passed on to us messages that others left for us on the phone. She was the one on whom we poured all our frustrations, disappointments, and pains. I lived with my parents until the age of thirty-eight.

After Sir Adrian Dingli, I went to teach at the higher secondary school in Naxxar, which is the equivalent of Sixth Form, with revision courses for those who failed their MATSEC exams, as well as courses preparing students for university entry. I taught both English and religion at this school. I loved teaching both. The higher secondary school was a great experience, particularly in the first years of my teaching there. I loved being with the young people. The students at the school were generally very approachable, had a certain humility about them, and were generally willing to relate to their teachers. On my part, I was ready to help anyone who asked for my help or who I thought I could support. My most memorable experiences were the time spent with the Highlighters. This was the name given to the Christian student community at the school. It was Helena Sammut who was mostly responsible for this group of students, but over the years, she was very much supported by Ruben Pace, Noel Bezzina, Mario Sciriha, and I. The Highlighters met during the midday break, during which time the students set about organizing the school liturgy, holding prayer meetings, and discussing various existential or religious themes, as well as organizing trips, excursions, and retreats for those who formed part of this group.

Around this time, I decided I would go back to university and do a master's degree. I knew that I could do it, and I felt a certain envy whenever someone would tell me that they were studying again, particularly when the studies were in theology. I just had to do it. I did start the course, but I never finished this degree. I did all the modules over the first two years, but never wrote the dissertation, which was meant to be written in the third year.

I was always in a rush during the academic year, especially between October and May. It was a crazy lifestyle. I would wake up early, go to daily mass, have breakfast, and drive to work. The school day would end at 3:00 p.m. I would come home, eat, have a shower, and leave the house again to pursue what I believed was my vocation. Most of my life was spent moving from one catechetical center to another. I would often have to make my own timetable: which town or village I would go to, what time I would be teaching, whom I would be addressing. There were times when I was invited by parishes to give talks to particular groups of parishioners: mothers of young children, parents of confirmands, and so on. No day was the same as the next. I worked very hard, and it was very stressful to fit everything in. Along with two other members, we would organize meetings and retreats for young people, so even my weekends were often taken up. We also created programs for different catechetical age groups. I was appreciated for my work, and I worked a lot. I did not know how to relax. Neither did I have the time to sit and chat. I wanted to make sure that a conversation would lead somewhere, otherwise I would not "waste" my time holding it.

This was a time when I was very task oriented. I hated inefficiency. I hated lack of action. I wanted to see things done and changes made. I wanted to be able to measure the results of my work, and I hated being surrounded by people who were slow to action or to change. I always felt that we were not doing enough; I complained that we were slumbering and that we ought to work harder, to be more vigorous, more zealous.

Some people would say that I am too demanding or too rigid. Other people would say that I am creative and colorful. I can be quite radical in my ideas. At the same time, I can be rigid concerning time and time lines, and I do not like changing plans that have already been established, or decisions that have been made. I hate what is old-fashioned while loving tradition. Of course, age and experience has taught me some flexibility. You could say that I am currently living from moment to moment, appreciating what beauty and life each moment brings.

In the summer of 1997, I did the full thirty-day Ignatian retreat at Mount St Joseph, Targa Gap, Mosta. My then spiritual director was Fr. Vince Magri, SJ, who ran the retreat center at the time and had a real vision for the retreat house as a center for Ignatian spirituality, and who was himself an experienced spiritual director. Before I started the retreat, Fr. Vince asked me to write down what it was that I desired from this retreat. I wrote in my journal that I wanted to be able to read and understand. I hoped to deepen my experience of God, to discover the nature of love, to be filled with this love. I wanted this retreat to give me the ability to offer myself generously to others. I desired a deep spiritual experience with Christ, and I was hoping that this would translate into action. I wanted Christ to do great things for me and with me. I hoped that as a consequence of this retreat, I would be able to communicate my love toward Christ when I spoke with others. I hoped that I would be filled with courage so that I would face everyday problems. I desired to feel God's presence from that moment onward, and also desired that I would always believe that I was loved by him. I hoped that I would never stop discerning whether I was doing his will. Finally, I hoped that I would feel his presence on my deathbed and that I would not be afraid of death—that I would be one with God at the moment of death.

I realize now that I was unrealistic and immature. Despite what I had read about the "dark night of the soul" Saint John of the Cross experienced,[3] I still hoped that I would be spared. Mother Teresa's *Come Be My Light: The Private Writings of the Saint of Calcutta*[4] had not as yet been published, and I still thought that with God life was always easier, which is not necessarily the case.

The Ignatian retreat was one of the central events in my spiritual life. I had been through various weekend retreats up till then, but they had all been focused mainly on preaching. I had never spent so much time on my own. As it turns out, the thirty-day retreat was a deep experience, with a flow of emotions ranging from sorrow, abandonment, despair to joy, adoration, and passion. I had become a member of the Society of Christian Doctrine in 1982, but what I had during this retreat was a real vocation, a real call. I was now more certain than ever that I belonged to God and that I would forever belong totally to him. From now on, I wanted to be completely his. I wanted every decision I made in the rest of my life to be approved and confirmed by him.

CHAPTER 3

The Crucified Christ Gazes upon Me

IN MARK 10:17–21, WE read:

> As he [Jesus] was setting out on a journey, a man ran up,
> knelt down before him, and asked him, "Good teacher,
> what must I do to inherit eternal life?" Jesus answered
> him, "Why do you call me good? No one is good but
> God alone. You know the commandments: 'You shall not
> kill; you shall not commit adultery; you shall not steal;
> you shall not bear false witness; you shall not defraud;
> honor your father and your mother." He replied and said
> to him, "Teacher, all of these I have observed from my
> youth." Jesus, looking at him, loved him.

In the book *Hearts on Fire: Praying with Jesuits*, edited by Michael Harter, John Eagan asks the following two questions: "How
do you, Lord, look at me? What do you feel in your heart for me?"[5]
I believe that the text from Mark answers our question. Is not the
phrase "Jesus looked steadily at him and he was filled with love for
him" amazing?

A. W. Tozer has said that our gaze upon God and God's gaze
upon us have the same effect. It is always heavenly. He writes:

> When we lift our inward eyes to gaze upon God we are
> sure to meet friendly eyes gazing back at us, for it is writ-
> ten that the eyes of the Lord run to and fro throughout
> all the earth. The sweet language of experience is "Thou

God seest me." When the eyes of the soul looking out meet the eyes of God looking in, heaven has begun right here on this earth."[6]

To be truly seen is one of the most significant experiences one can ever have, just as to be invisible to others—to be totally ignored by others—can be destructive, heartbreaking, and deeply painful. To have an experience where you are truly seen by God, to have God gaze at you, is deeply comforting and profoundly healing. Realizing that God sees you and knowing that God's loving gaze is upon you is a truly transformative experience. To be noticed, to be seen, to be truly known and accepted, to be truly loved is therapeutic. Is that not what all of us desire? The experience of being gazed upon by someone who loves us and whom we love in return is amazing. Knowing that God loves us deeply is one of the greatest soul-healing realizations we can ever have.

In my case, it was Christ's gaze that I experienced. And in my case, it was while he was on the cross that he saw me. It was there that his gaze followed me. It was in that gaze, which was penetrating, knowing, and benign, that I found the deepest joy and the most profound wisdom. That was the first time I felt that I had truly been seen.

In his book *Under the Gaze of God: Perspectives on Spiritual Development*, G. David Williams describes a mother's gaze as "all-absorbing; exclusive; filled with wonder and love; tranquil; and protective."[7] That is precisely what Christ's gaze felt like at that particular moment. Christ had looked at me in the same way that my mother must have gazed at me when I was still an infant at her breast. It was a tender gaze. Christ's gaze was not fleeting. It was not just a swift glance. It lasted. I could see Christ's head turning toward me as I walked in and out of his vision amongst the crowd. This was an experience of compassionate love.

I was thirty-three years old when I decided that I wanted to do something out of the ordinary for my thirty-third year. This desire was inspired by a romantic spirituality arising out of the emphasis on Christ's death at the age of thirty-three. I decided I would do the Ignatian exercises over the summer holidays. My intention was to come under the gaze of God, to open my heart to God's scrutiny, to go over my life and my plans and my relationships in God's presence. And I did. Just after my thirty-fourth birthday. This was 1997, and that is when I experienced the gaze of the Crucified Christ.

I had been on retreat for twenty-four days. This was the third week of the spiritual exercises, and I was not only experiencing the abandonment of God but feeling very abandoned myself. In the previous meditations, I had felt ignored by Christ. It seemed to me that Christ was burdened by his own calling: suffering on the cross was such a heavy load he was having to bear that I felt he had no time, strength, or vitality for me. I was frustrated at myself for being so needy. I wanted to be with him. I wanted to be there for him. But I also wanted him to be with me, to be there for me. For hours, I stayed with Christ in the Garden of Gethsemane. I knelt alongside him or watched him from afar. I watched his despair. I watched his blood draining from his body. I saw his matted hair. His inner turmoil was tangible. And yet, although I yearned to be with him, it seemed as if he could not see me. He manifested no consciousness of my presence.

And then it happened. On the twenty-fifth day of the retreat. I was contemplating the death of Christ on the cross. And the meditation started with me imagining that I was part of the crowd. I was not standing still in this contemplation. I was walking in and out of Christ's view. And Christ was looking at me steadily and following my movement. It was the gaze of a dying man, his eyes swollen, his face dripping blood. His gaze was loving, but full of pain. It became clear there and then that God desired me to be with him. He wanted time with me at the moment when he was most vulnerable. He wanted to die with me watching him, loving him. He desired to experience his death with me being present for him. He wanted my thoughts, my feelings, my body to follow him, just as he was following me with his vision. I could see his head hanging to one side. He was close to death. In my mind and heart, Christ was not saying any of the famous last words which we find in the Gospel, but his gaze was loving, yearning, calling.

I had been trying to be with God, to gaze at God, to feel his presence, and I realized that God was one step before me: he wanted to be with me, to gaze at me—he wanted to feel my presence. He wanted me to experience him at the moment of his vulnerability. Christ was telling me that I was so accepted that he wanted me to be with him at his most fragile moment. God was extending a special welcome to me. In the opinion of some, I would always remain an "unpolished" woman, and in the opinion of others, I would always be remembered as one born into a social class that is as vile as the shepherds mentioned in the Gospels. To Christ, the opinion of others did not count. Even my sin, my ambition, and my anger did not count.

Jesus simply said: "Pauline, stay where I can see you." What a strange and mysterious command! I am certain to this day that these words could not have come from inside of me, in the sense that I could not have invented these words myself, knowing the frame of mind I was in. I felt too abandoned by my own God to come up with words that felt so intimate. At the same time, these words could not have come from outside of me. I heard them with my inner senses, but heard them loud and clear. I have, since then, spent years trying to comprehend these words, and I often come back to them in my meditation and my prayers. But the voice was very clear.

The statement "Stay where I can see you" could have been an invitation to prayer, to be in his presence on that day. It could also have been Christ's way of asking the question he had asked Peter: "Do you love me?" His answer for me was not "Feed my sheep" (see John 21:15–17) but rather "Stay where I can see you"—that is, remain close to me. Do not hide from me. Let me be present in your life. Do not let anyone or anything get between us. Do not let anything or anyone hide me from you or hide you from my vision. In *The Shaking of the Foundations*," the theologian Paul Tillich writes:

> Grace strikes us when we are in great pain and restlessness. It strikes us when we walk through the dark valley of a meaningless and empty life. It strikes us when we feel that our separation is deeper than usual, because we have violated another life, a life which we loved, or from which we were estranged. It strikes us when our disgust for our own being, our indifference, our weakness, our hostility, and our lack of direction and composure have

become intolerable to us. It strikes us when, year after year, the longed-for perfection of life does not appear, when the old compulsions reign within us as they have for decades, when despair destroys all joy and courage. Sometimes at that moment a wave of light breaks into our darkness, and it is as though a voice were saying: You are accepted. You are accepted, accepted by that which is greater than you, and the name of which you do not know. Do not ask for the name now; perhaps you will find it later. Do not try to do anything now; perhaps later you will do much. Do not seek for anything; do not perform anything; do not intend anything. Simply accept the fact that you are accepted![8]

The loving gaze of Christ revealed to me God's desire for time with me; God's appreciation of me; God's acceptance of the whole of me, including my thoughts and feelings; and God's desire to experience me, to always have me by his side.

This statement could also be interpreted as a commitment on the part of God to protect me. "Stay where I can see you" could have meant what it means when a mother or a carer tells his or her child to stay in their view, to not go anywhere he or she cannot be watched. In this case, Christ would have been expressing his care for me. He would also have set some responsibility onto me: asking me to ensure that I do not drift away from his presence. According to this latter interpretation, Christ was once again asking me to remain in his line of vision.

Thirdly, Christ could have been saying that my presence was a consolation to him at a time when he was alone, broken, and humiliated. Did he really want me to be with him? Was he actually identifying me from the crowd and electing me to be closer to him? Did he actually expect me to be a consolation for him? Could my existence and presence console God? If God really wanted me to console him, like Thérèse of Lisieux did, it was a huge vocation that I was being called to. Was I really capable of it? I had to admit that I very rarely fulfilled my vocation of being a consolation for God. That is, there have not been very many times when I sought to please him, to let him be rested in me, rather than seeking God's consolations. Most of the time I request his comfort and solace, ask him for his comfort and solace, ask him for his peace, and beg him for courage, for his love and for his forgiveness, rather than wishing to soothe him and to serve as a restful place for him.

Finally, Christ could have been telling me that he did not want my work—he wanted me. He said, "Stay," not "Do"! I realized that my hectic lifestyle was not necessarily bringing me closer to God and that I had turned into a spiritual workaholic.

I am now in my late fifties. And yet, Christ's gaze from the cross is still as vivid in my memory as on that day in 1997. I have relived that experience over and over in my memory, and I have tried to understand it in the different circumstances in which I have found myself.

Life continued after the Ignatian retreat.

Coming out of the retreat, I bought my first property. This was one of the decisions that I had made during the Ignatian retreat. It was what we call a maisonette—that is, a building with a private entrance that occupies the first floor and has another maisonette belonging to different owners right above it. I also bought a garage close by. It was in shell form—no electricity or plumbing, just limestone and bricks—when I bought it, and I had to make a lot of sacrifices in order to finish and furnish it. I did not intend to leave home at the time, but when it was finished in the year 2000, I decided that I would move out of my parents' home and move into this building. It was a hard decision. Probably as hard as that of Thérèse Martin—that is, of Thérèse of Lisieux—when she left her father's home. But I had to do it. My mother's house was always busy, with people coming and going all the time and the television always blaring. I needed space, I needed silence, I needed creativity, I needed freedom. It was hard financially to find the money to pay for the plastering, the windows and doors, the floor tiles, the bathrooms. But this made me feel human. Most people have to go through this financial burden in trying to provide a home for their family. I guess that having to pay my way alone was slightly harder, but then again, so many men and women who are separated have to start from scratch. Above all, it was hard emotionally. I love my mother. My brother Reno was married that same year, and my mother ended up with just my younger brother Christopher in the home. Chris left home over a decade later.

Having my own place has also given me a lot of joy and a sense of freedom. The satisfaction that one gets out of buying a piece of property is huge. Having my own property helped me express my creativity. I could design my place as I wanted it, invite whoever I wished into the house, own pets if I wanted. Having my own place made me feel much freer, but also more creative. I have grown plants, restored furniture, painted and repainted rooms, created reading corners. Twenty years later, I signed another contract. This time, I bought a small flat in Buġibba where I could spend my summers, close to the water and to the promenade. This may seem like capitalism. It could be. However, I have to say that this flat has made it possible for me to once again design a nice space for myself. It has given me a place to go to when I felt lonely, stressed, and broken.

Fr. Vince came back with a proposition some time after the Ignatian retreat. He intended to create a course which would train laypeople to be spiritual directors. That was the first time such an opportunity had arisen. Spiritual direction had, up till then, only been provided by priests. This was not the case within the SDC. Saint George Preca had been forward-looking in this regard. He had wanted lay members of the Society to seek spiritual direction from another lay member of his or her section within the Society, and for those within the Society who were asked to serve as spiritual directors to accept to help their comembers. I had been giving spiritual direction within the SDC for a few years, and Fr. Vince's proposition was really welcome. I accepted. The other people participating in the course were just amazing. This was a really powerful time spiritually. I was studying Ignatian spirituality, I was constantly in the company of people who were taking their spiritual lives seriously, I had a mentor in the course who was there to suggest readings for me and to answer my queries, and the lectures were really of very high quality and very deep.

In the year 1999, I was called by Archbishop Mercieca to be a member of the central commission of the pastoral synod. It was an adventure that went on till 2003. It was a very enriching experience while it lasted, in the sense that I got to know a lot of people,

I learned a lot about the structure of the local church, and there was always something challenging to discuss. I felt that I was doing something for the church in Malta, and I felt very important. We met once every fortnight at the diocesan curia in Floriana. Later on, I also got involved with one of the working groups. The group writing the document on culture and society was finding it difficult to finalize their document. The group consisted of some of the best brains on the island: Rev. Prof. Serracino Inglott, Rev. Dr. Rene Camilleri, Dr. John Cachia, Rev. Jimmy Bartolo, SJ, Prof. Anthony Frendo, and Prof. Stanley Fiorini. I only had two or three meetings with them, but what an honor to be part of that group.

And then, right in the middle of this glorious time, my nervous breakdown struck. I had been working without a break for many years. My studies, my work with the SDC, my work with the synod, my course in spiritual direction. My body just gave in. I could not sleep, I could not eat, I had constant palpitations, and I suffered from exhaustion. It was horrible. I did all sorts of tests, and it was clear that my illness was stress related. I was told that I had depression. I resented this diagnosis. I was never really sad. I went to the psychiatrist Dr. David Cassar, who told me that I had an anxiety disorder. That was the first time I had been to the psychiatrist and the first time I had heard of this condition. He gave me antidepressants. I took it as a humiliation. When I thought I had reached the peak of my success, of recognition, my legs were suddenly cut from under me. Thank goodness, I did get over that crisis through the help of some medication and psychotherapy that gave me my confidence back. But it took me a whole year.

In September 2005, I left Malta to go to the UK. I had no return ticket. I was quite willing to settle there for good. Malta had, I felt, become too small for me. I ended up teaching religious education (RE) in a school in Reading. I loved the freedom that I experienced during this year. This was the first time I felt free enough to lie down on the grass in the park. I finally got to ride a bicycle, something I had never done in Malta. I was only thirty minutes away from London, and I loved traveling on trains during the weekend. Sometimes, I would travel to Kent and spend the weekend at my brother's, which was nice. The experience of teaching was immensely enriching, but I cannot say that it was easy. The culture shock was obvious, and I lacked the jargon that would have made me relevant to the young people I taught at the Elvian School.

Studying abroad was a dream I'd always had, but I could never see myself affording it. However, by the end of that year in Reading, I had saved enough money to stay over in the UK for another year as a full-time student in London. I applied to do an MTh at Heythrop College, the Jesuit college that formed part of the University of London. I would be living in London for the next year. I started my MTh at Heythrop in September 2005.

And now comes the fiery part of my story. My friend X and I met in Brixton Parish in London in 2006. He was a priest. He had given a wonderful talk about the Eucharist, and I asked to speak to him after that. That was the first meeting which sealed our friendship. It was March 2006. We fell in love almost instantly. I knew he was my soul mate, and I was his. During my time in London, we were inseparable. We went to libraries, visited museums, prayed, and shared all our hopes and our thoughts. It was with him that I watched the unforgettable *Les Misérables*.

Six months after our first meeting, I had to return to Malta. After that, we kept in touch through emails, through Skype, and through phone calls. Although we lived in different countries, we supported each other emotionally and psychologically. I supported him while he did his PhD, and then he supported me while I did mine. I met him a few more times over the years. I visited him in London at his alma mater and in his home country, whereas he made the trip to Malta. Whenever we met, we were always immensely happy in each other's company. It was a relationship that filled me with joy, but also with fear and guilt. I was forty-two, and there I was, falling in love for the first time in my life.

It is very difficult to descibe the agony involved when someone who has been a celibate all his or her life suddenly finds him- or herself head over heels in love with someone. In this case, this someone was also a celibate person. I was full of guilt, and there were times when I felt physically ill with fear, when I lost all appetite and could not eat, and when I was filled with shame. I had written a journal of the whole of our relationship, but I deleted all documents and photos related to him when I decided, upon my return to Malta, that it was best not to pursue this friendship. I wanted to destroy all the documents and photos related to him not because I was afraid other people might be able to access them but because I did not wish to be reminded of him, since he had wreaked havoc in my life. His emails were frequent, and they were always rich with descriptions of what he had been doing, what he had been reading, and what his emotions were telling him. I loved him for it. I thought I would share with you one email which still remains in my inbox. He sent it to me on May 24, 2006, just a few weeks after our first meeting. It reads:

> Dear Pauline, the profound innocence that [typifies] our friendship, such as in appreciating the flowers together this afternoon, is simply very sweet. It was a memory I carried with me all day long, and now that I am preparing to retire to bed it struck me deeply as something, among other things, to be thankful to God for. Why are we struggling with ourselves on a daily basis when there is so much to be thankful to God for in this friendship? It is a rhetorical question, because my own struggle now rekindles the long-standing doubt about whether I am, and could become, the really perfect person that I've so frequently yearned to be. Apparently, many of us who are celibate subconsciously blame ourselves for giving and receiving love from another person, or feel confused about how we can love God and another person in any intense sense. I think this arises from leading parallel lives, an external life that takes its natural course in the ministries we do, and an internal life where our deep feelings remain concealed to the rest of the world and fully revealed to the Lord. To love another person in more than an ordinary way is, as it were, to expose ourselves to a sense of vulnerability, or even to take the risk of being misunderstood. As children our lives were filled with friends, fun, learning and doing . . . innocence was a hallmark of that phase. The internal life was filled with childish uncertainty, doubt, even anger and the dread of [the] ever-looming unknown. No one can parallel life with an absolute knowledge of triumphs that will take

place. In the context of our friendship as matured adults, there is both a rational coherence of the external/internal and the affective dilemma as to whether we are doing this "love thing" right. In experiencing the manifold beauties that this friendship enfolds like petals of a flower on a day to day basis let's continue to merge the best in our minds and spirit, in the continuing dependence on God for our strength. Pedro Arrupe wrote a poem about love just before his death in the late 1980s, which I have often read, but reading it now enlarges the meaning:*

"Fall in Love"
Nothing is more practical than
finding God, than
falling in Love
in a quite absolute, final way.
What you are in love with,
what seizes your imagination, will affect everything.
It will decide
what will get you out of bed in the morning,
what you do with your evenings,
how you spend your weekends,
what you read, whom you know,
what breaks your heart,
and what amazes you with joy and gratitude.
Fall in Love, stay in love,
and it will decide everything."[9]

In another email sent to me a few days later, on May 31, he wrote:

I have been thinking about us since the noble beginning of our friendship. But following the events of two nights ago, I have thought more about it and these are my truncated reflections for now. No doubt, it is a beautiful friendship in my experience; that, I guess, is the reason for this trajectory of emotional intimacy, where the warmth of a supportive, affectionate, passionate bonding takes place between us. The meeting of two hearts. Every meeting between us offers us a place where hopes, fears,

* My friend sent me a different version of this poem, but here I have cited the more official version.

dreams, secrets feel safe to, as it were, emerge. Your, and of course, my heart reveals something and is met with a truthful and compassionate response of another heart. If the Thames could speak to us in the words of a human being, it would probably have a thing or two about our serene walks, our quiet heartbeats, our timid sighs, our veiled fears, our definite hopes, our hushed hesitations, our tentative letting go, our blissful laughter, our hidden tears, our soothing joys, our muted sadness, our understood language of silence, our shared admiration for its beauty . . . by its banks. Pauline, I am sorry that I am not as strong as I usually am. I wish I were, for you!

I returned to Malta in September 2006, and went back to the UK for my graduation in December of that same year. It was clear to me that I was going to find living my celibacy very difficult if I stayed in touch. This was the closest I had come to intimacy. For the first time in my life, at the age of forty-two, I loved someone completely and unconditionally, and I was loved back with the same depth of love. He did not care that I wore spectacles, that my hips were too wide. He adored me as much as I adored him. He was a lawyer as well as a priest, and a theoretician as well as an activist in human rights, and there were times when we walked the streets of London till 3:00 a.m. in the morning, just talking about things. What a joy it was! The time just flew by, and we would find that we had spent six hours in what seemed like a couple of minutes.

In January 2007, I wrote an email to him from Malta, stating that I would like to break up our relationship. In the meantime, I went into a desperate rant, destroying the emails and the photos that I had of him. I wanted to forget him completely. He had given me unconditional love but had also put me into the worst turmoil. I was meant to belong to God alone, and here I was enraptured and completely fixated on this man.

He contacted me some weeks later, claiming that he had been diagnosed with liver cancer. Despite this news, I wished to persevere in my decision: no contact at all. It was a very difficult and lonely year for me. In September 2007, I decided that I had to get back to him. The silence between us had been eating me on the inside. I did get back to him. I did so because I was still obsessed by him, because I was worried about his health, and because I felt that I had done him a terrible misdeed abandoning him in that manner, and at a time when he was ill in a foreign country. I was guilt ridden. We spoke for hours. He told me about the pain he went through after I had abandoned him and while he was being treated for his cancer. I tried to explain why I had done what I did. We both had to forgive each other, and we did. We both agreed that marriage was not what we wanted, but also that our friendship was not to be relinquished, either. As I wrote earlier, we met a couple of times after this in different countries until his death in December 2015. He died in a car crash.

When he died, I was devastated. This was no romance scam. The hardest thing to bear was the fact that I had no one I could share my grief with. This was someone who had loved me enough to propose marriage to me. It was someone whose marriage proposal I would have accepted had it not been for my previous vocational commitment. I would have loved to spend the rest of my life with him. At the same time, I am so glad that I was faithful to my original calling.

I knew one of his closest friends, and I asked him to do me a favor. At one time, Fr. X and I had been to a museum in London where one of the exhibits consisted of a beautiful quote from Raymond Carver. Fr. X had really loved this quote and had taken a photo of me with this quote in the background. I sent this to his friend by email and asked this friend to print it out and to have it buried with him. The words read:

> And did you get what
> you wanted from this life, even so?
> I did.
> And what did you want?
> To call myself beloved, to feel myself
> beloved on the earth.[10]

I found out about the accident on Saturday, December 26, 2015, through an email which an American friend of his sent to me. I had texted him on Christmas day, wishing him all the best, not knowing that he was already gone. Obviously, he did not reply. Reading the news of the accident was a huge shock to me. Fr. X and myself had often spoken about the possibility of one of us dying, and had wondered how the other would find out about it, but I certainly did not expect to lose his friendship so soon. Fr. X was seven years my junior, and I never expected him to die before I did.

As I said, I was devastated, especially because I was going through the toughest patch within the SDC, where I was feeling unloved. I knew I would miss him dreadfully, because that depth of communication could not be duplicated. I told myself that I should be grateful for the ten years of friendship that we had, but we were soul mates, and I sorely missed our conversations, our emails, and his encouraging and hope-filled phone calls. Above all, I missed his authenticity. He was so sincere and so truthful. And he was such a great teacher. But then, death is definite, and there is no use crying . . . I just had to accept that he was gone.

Upon his death, I wrote an email to his father. I did not know his address, and I sent the email to a friend who did. I wrote the following: "If it is any consolation to you, I adored your son. He had such gentleness, such wisdom. I thought of him and prayed for him every single day, and I did everything I could to support him. I was blessed because he 'adored' me as much as I did him. I looked up to him as so much better than myself. And, quite amazingly, he did the same."

His funeral was held at his university, with close to a thousand in attendance. And that was it. That was the end of my love story. In a way, I felt relieved. I could continue to get on with my life. My love for him had filled me with too much guilt, and along with the joy of being loved and being in love, there was always the shame that I felt that I was living a double life—that this was not how celibacy should be lived, that celibacy required a total immersion in God, my Original Lover, and that I should have been totally focused on him.

Fr. Arthur Vella, SJ, knew everything. It was with him that I shared the frustration, the despair, and the joys of this relationship. Turu, as Fr. Arthur was called, was one of those priests—a Jesuit, in fact—who understood the fragility of humanity. Everyone felt comfortable sharing with him whatever it was that disturbed him or her. He dedicated most of his life to spiritual direction, and he was truly wonderful at it. Everyone just loved him, including myself. He loved the Jesuits and knew their history; he loved the local church and was always up to date on what was happening in the diocese; he loved each and every consecrated individual on the island, whether priest, brother, nun, or layperson. He had this ability to listen that was quite exceptional. He was never judgmental, and he could truly heal the soul. He died on my birthday—that is, on May 20, 2018—at the age of eighty-seven years.

During those two years when I was in the UK, I was in close contact with the male members of the Society, who, at that time, were still residing at the presbytery of the Our Lady of the Rosary parish, in Brixton. During the first year I was working in Reading, I would visit London on alternate weekends and join the members in their assigned meetings, or else would participate in events organized by them, such as the confirmation class on Saturday or the meeting of the Maltese migrant group on Sundays. The following year, when I was in London doing my master's in theology at Heythrop, I lived within walking distance from the MUSEUM center. I lived on Sudbourne Road and would simply walk down Brixton Hill to the presbytery. During this time, I learned to appreciate even further the structure and the style of the Society. And I found out a lot about my own family back home, from Wiġi, or Louis, the oldest member of the Society in the UK, who was also from my home town and who had known my paternal grandfather, Frinu.

When I returned to Malta in 2006, I was asked to run a MUSEUM center with around seventy-five children. The children were lovely, and the parents were great. But I was lonely. There were three other members at my center, two of them older than seventy-five years. It was tough. Having had that wonderful relationship with my friend abroad, I felt more alone than ever. There was the struggle of living the solitude that is required of a celibate life and the easy solution of a phone call. I could just call him, and he would understand. At this time, he was doing his doctorate, but he knew what community life could be like and how lonely it could be. I was only at this center for one year. The following year, I was transferred to another, bigger center with more children, more parents, and a younger team. I gave my all—my time, my resources, my creativity, my love. However, a new member joined the team in the second year, and there were clashes every day. Suddenly, I was isolated. Some of the members would not even speak to me, and none of them had the guts to tell me what was wrong, what I was doing wrong, and why things had turned so rancid. It was just horrible. The others would go to lunch as a group and not even tell me about it, let alone invite me to join. This was really painful. The practice within the SDC is that if you work as a catechist and a member in a particular center, you also spend your free time together with the other members as a community. I was being completely boycotted. We would organize an event for parents and children, and none of the others would turn up on time. They would turn up thirty or forty-five minutes after the beginning of a one-hour event and have me be there on my own. Once again, I felt that I was experiencing, along with Christ, the abandonment of Christ in the Garden of Gethsemane and on the cross.

It is strange to speak of members of a voluntary religious organization doing this to each other, but my God, we did. My prayers at the time were prayers in which I joined Jesus in the Garden of Gethsemane, suffering the depth of abandonment. The worst time was Lent of 2010. I knelt alongside Christ in that garden for most of my waking hours, because the experience had really affected the whole of me. It gave me such a sense of exasperation and so much sorrow. What a painful experience it was for me. I sometimes felt that society in general was holy in comparison with the members of the SDC, with its promise of holiness. Of course, I have always believed that as long as we are alive, none of us can pretend to be holy, but this was such a harsh experience for me that I felt I was practically being attacked by the evil one.

Saint George Preca was to be canonized by Pope Benedict XVI on June 3, 2007. There were various activities organized by SDC which were meant to prepare the members of the Society for this event, and I have some beautiful memories of both sections of the Society gathered in prayer or celebration. Hundreds of Maltese flocked to Rome for the canonization ceremony at St Peter's Square,

Vatican City, including myself. But the actual day was a total disappointment. It rained heavily, and we were completely drenched. It was difficult to focus on the ceremony when even your underwear was dripping wet!

In the meantime, I was once again teaching at the higher secondary school. However, having returned from my London experience, teaching at this school was torture. I was often given the classes which no one else wanted—or rather, the least-appreciated courses. My life was just too boring, and boredom can kill the spirit. I wanted more. I had made some lasting friendships at this school, but I felt uncomfortable with most of the other members of the teaching staff. It felt totally unchallenging, and I started looking for a way out. I thought that I had gotten tired of teaching, so I applied for the position of education officer within the education division. I had twenty years of teaching experience and was hoping that this role would allow me to influence the way religious education was done in schools in Malta. This was a position which would allow me to visit schools while giving me a say as to the nature, structure, and content of religious education. Up until then, it was always a Catholic priest who had fulfilled that role. So, in accepting the post, I would be the first layperson to become an education officer for religious education in schools.

In the meantime, there was also a vacancy at the junior college for a full-time lecturer in religious knowledge, and I applied for that as well. When I got this job as well, I had to decide. I resigned from the post of education officer and took on the teaching post of lecturer at the junior college. I am so glad I did. I realize now that I would have made very little headway with religious education within the education division. There are too many competing political interests, and my contribution would have had little effect. That position would only have exasperated me.

One summer, I visited the Holy Land: Bethlehem, Nazareth, and Jerusalem. Our bus arrived in Jerusalem late one evening. I wept when I saw the walls of Jerusalem. But it was the Holy Sepulchre that most affected me. Tourists and pilgrims flock to the place, and they do not keep an ordered line. When I was there, people were pushing and shoving to try and get inside the tomb before everyone else. It was very unpleasant, and there was nothing devotional about it. However, once the pilgrim finds him- or herself inside the tomb, the import of the moment, the sanctity of the space, just hit him. Well, it hit me. I went to confession in the chapel dedicated to Mary Magdalene. The priest was from Brazil. He could speak Italian and understand some English, whereas I could speak English and understood Italian. It was one of the most beautiful sacramental confessions I ever experienced, even though we struggled with the verbal communication. I spoke about the turmoil in my emotional life, and at the end of it all, this priest gave me this really generous, heartwarming hug that reflected God's complete forgiveness.

I started teaching at the junior college in October of 2008. I was there until the summer of 2014. It was a joy being in the presence of all those intelligent young people. I did not have too many friends from among the staff because time was short, but I made some very deep friendships and I was reunited with an ex-student of mine: Emanuel Buttigieg, who had returned from Cambridge with a doctorate in history.

In 2009, I started thinking about carrying on with my own theological studies. I started my communications with Professor Paul Murray at Durham University in the UK. I wanted to do something on the saints or on the authority of the saints. Professor Murray suggested that I spend a year reading into the subject before actually applying. I realized that if I wanted to write about the saints and about their authority within the church, there were two theologians that I could use: Hans Urs von Balthasar or Cardinal John Henry Newman. In the end, when I started in September of 2010, I thought I could compare Balthasar with the Austrian-British philosopher Ludwig Wittgenstein. I thought I could use the coherence theory of truth to argue that the authority of the saints arose from the fact that they were bearers of truth values which cohered with Christian principles. I had read some of Wittgenstein's work when I was at Heythrop, and I thought that this was a good proposal. I was accepted as a doctoral student at Durham, but my supervisor would not be Professor Paul Murray but instead Professor Mark Allen MacIntosh.

Professor MacIntosh was a great supervisor. He insisted right from the start that the doctorate had to be doable and that I should focus on Hans Urs von Balthasar alone, and leave Wittgenstein out of the picture. I am so glad I took his advice.

I was not in Durham for long stretches, since I was doing my PhD part-time. But whenever I was there, Professor MacIntosh would make sure that he made time for me. He would not only see me but would also invite me to his home, along with other students of his. We would discuss our research, ask questions, and give feedback on each other's work. Mark Allen MacIntosh was the Van Mildert Professor of Divinity at Durham University, but also a canon residentiary of Durham Cathedral. His beautiful home was just beyond the cathedral, within the cathedral precinct. For someone like myself, the Durham experience had all the romantic elements anyone could wish for. I was a member of University College, which meant that Durham Castle was my college. Durham Cathedral, which held the relics of Saint Cuthbert and Venerable Bede, was just across Palace Green. Also on the green was the Department of Theology and Religion, where I had my meetings with Professor Paul Murray, my second supervisor.

My doctoral research would focus on the authority of the saints within the church. There were two things which captivated me. Firstly, the fact that history is full of examples of individuals who held positions of official authority which they did not deserve. Secondly, the way in which philosophical and theological trends have an impact—not just on the process leading to the canonization of a saint but also on the esteem with which a saint is held and on the perpetuation of, or the decrease in, the veneration toward that saint. I explored whether, and to what extent, we may attribute authority to the saints, but also how we may ensure that it is the saints, and not the scoundrels, whose influence persists and whose memory endures. I was convinced that Hans Urs von Balthasar could help us clarify the issues surrounding the authority of the saints. Besides establishing Balthasar's involvement with the enterprise, my research tried to establish the theological foundations upon which the authority of the saints would have to be based. I argued that, in practice, the saints already act as the final authority, but the foundations of this authority are yet to be argued theoretically.

In September 2014, I signed a contract with the University of Malta. I was to be a full-time resident academic within the faculty of theology. I was hoping that I would finally get the opportunity to read all the books I meant to read and to write what I had learned throughout my half a century of life, and my close to thirty years work experience. But it took me a long time to learn the legal framework and the procedures of the institution, and although it was not something I wanted to happen, I still found myself embroiled in the politics of the place. To my dismay, I realized that success as an academic was less about loving and mentoring one's students, and more about selling and marketing oneself.

I defended my dissertation on April 1, 2015, and graduated in June of that same year. My book detailing the conclusions of my study was published in 2017. Each one of these events was a joyful experience. Unfortunately, there were not too many people who celebrated my success, and I felt as if my circle of friends became smaller when I got my doctorate. Certainly, one friend who stayed by my side and always encouraged me on was Fr. Joe Inguanez, a Catholic priest and sociologist who always gave me wise advice when it came to my career and my research.

CHAPTER 4

To Gaze at God

IN *THE PURSUIT OF God*, A. W. Tozer has a whole essay called "The Gaze of the Soul," where he turns to the metaphor of sight, challenging us to a new kind of seeing. It is not the kind of seeing that is content to simply identify or occasionally recognize God's presence. Rather, it is the kind of seeing where we are encouraged to develop the lover's gaze—that unmistakable look of a soul that has completely lost itself in another person.[11]

The beautiful thing is that once I located that Face, so to speak, I realized that that Face was seeking my face just as much as I was seeking his. The thing with seeing another person looking at you is that you, too, have to be looking at him or her in order to realize that their gaze is in your direction. I can only see God gazing at me if I am already gazing at him. If you are to know whether God's gaze is still there, you have to keep your own gaze steadily in his direction. You have to be willing to seek his face, to steadfastly return his gaze. Augustine speaks of the *videntem videre*—that is, he emphasizes that God's gaze is prior to ours, that we are already known by God before we know him, and that we get to know God by letting him look at us. Meister Eckhart (ca. 1260–1328) writes of the mystical union that occurs in the gaze between God and the mystic: "The eye with which I see God is the same eye with which God sees me: my eye and God's eye are one eye, one seeing, one knowing and one love."[12]

In the fifth chapter of *De Visione Dei*, Nicholas of Cusa (1401–64) emphasizes the kenotic nature of God, who allows us to see his face:

> Lord, when you look upon me with an eye of graciousness, what is your seeing, other than your being seen by me? In seeing me, you who are *deus absconditus* give yourself to be seen by me. No one can see you except insofar as you grant that you be seen. To see you is not other than that you see the one who sees you. By means of this icon of you, O Lord, I see how favorably disposed you are to show your face to all who seek you. For you never close your eyes; you never turn [them] away. And although I turn away from you when I completely turn to something else, you do not on this account change your eyes or your gaze. If you do not look upon me with an eye of grace, it is my fault, because I am separated from you through my turning away and through my turning toward something else, which I prefer to you. Notwithstanding, you still do not turn altogether away from me, but your mercy follows me in case at some time I might wish to turn back to you in order to be capable of receiving your grace.[13]

In *Seeing the Form*, the Swiss theologian Hans Urs von Balthasar writes:

> Man's vision of God is like an echo of the antecedent and foundational event of being seen by God—so much an echo that man's longing to see God can come to rest in the consciousness of being seen by God and can renounce any self-vision which is divorced from this being-seen-by-God or rather may come to understand that his vision of God is included in his being seen by God.[14]

There is a beautiful para-liturgical ceremony within the Society of Christian Doctrine written by the founder, Saint George Preca. I was seventeen years old when I underwent this ceremony. It is a ceremony that one undergoes because it is a kind of ceremony of initiation, the undertaking of a new responsibility. The ceremony has two beautiful moments. One of them is when the candidate looks at the crucifix and states: "I resolve to look upon you alone for the rest of my life." This is taken to mean by some that the person is choosing to remain in the SDC, thus promising to remain celibate. However, this could have been inspired by "The Meditation on the Two Standards" that one finds in Ignatius of Loyola's spiritual exercises. Choosing the Standard of Christ and choosing Christ as one's teacher is a confirmation of the sacraments of baptism and confirmation, and not necessarily a religious vocation. The other significant moment takes place when the superior holds the crucifix with both arms, presenting it to those present, and intones a litany consisting of a list of titles and attributes that are assigned to Christ. This is called the *Mons Domini* and is based on the Beatitudes: Jesus is presented as the humble teacher, as the meek teacher, and so on and so forth.

My own mystical experience during the Ignatian retreat must have actually been a mere deepening or reliving of my first commitment to Christ. When I was still in my teens, I had already promised that I would look at no one but him crucified. My experience during the retreat reminded me that his gaze was there to receive mine. And my own experience of human love has taught me even further how amazing a love gaze can be. Two people staring into each other's eyes can be a sign of true love.

Saint George Preca once had a very powerful mystical experience. He called it "the extraordinary vision of the child Jesus." He narrates how one morning he was walking close to the Marsa Cross (*Is-Salib tal-Marsa*), when he suddenly noticed a boy pushing a cart and holding a bag of manure. The boy fixed his gaze on George and imperiously ordered him to lend him a hand. The instant Fr. George held the handles of the cart, he experienced an extraordinary spiritual sweetness. So deep was this experience that Fr. George could never recall what had happened after that—that is, where they had gone or what had happened to the young boy. But he later came to the realization that the boy was Jesus, and that Jesus had been asking him and his followers for help. George Preca often revisited this experience and narrated it over and over again to the members of the Society, claiming that they had been helping him push the cart.[15]

In my case, too, I have had to revisit the words which I heard Jesus say: "Stay where I can see you." For me, too, the voice was very clear. In my case also, I have had to interpret these words in different ways over time: I realize now that the same words could also mean "Stay where you can see me."

The challenges never stop. In September of 2016, Graziella Buttigieg, Margaret Santucci, and I started planning a pilgrimage to Santiago de Compostela. Almost every evening, rain or shine, you would see three women and a dog walking across the Victoria Lines from Naxxar to Gharghur. It was very tough, for me in particular. I really had to start building my muscle from scratch.

The trip took twelve days, and we walked for ten of those twelve days. We decided to walk the Portuguese Way, along the coast for the first few days, and then up hills, down valleys, and through forests and towns that made each and every vista worth the effort. On the last day, approaching Santiago de Compostela in the evening was a real struggle. We could barely lift our feet. But we made it, and what a feeling of exhilaration as we approached the cathedral that evening! The following day, when we went for Sunday mass and saw the swinging of the incense, this feeling of achievement grew. I felt rejuvenated, energized. I was certain I heard God's voice telling me: "I want so much more from you." The physical challenge had been much more than I had ever thought myself capable of, and I felt that there was so much more I could do for God.

In mid-December of 2019, I started realizing that something was wrong with my body. I was in quite a bit of pain. I had a very bad itch on the right side of my abdomen, which hurt with every breath. I also had a low fever for a couple of days. Furthermore, I had what seemed like a bad panic attack, with palpitations and a semi-blackout. I decided I would go to Mosta Health Centre just two miles down the hill from my home. A chest X-ray showed no sign of infection. The doctor, however, sent me to the emergency room at the island's main hospital, Mater Dei, primarily because of the fever. Blood tests were carried out at Mater Dei. The CRP level in the blood was high. I was given antibiotics and painkillers by the doctor at the emergency room and was told to visit the family doctor after a few days. I did visit my general practitioner in Naxxar:

Dr. Debbie Formosa St John. That was Thursday, December 19. Her first diagnosis was gallstones. She sent me to a private clinic for an ultrasound, as well as for blood tests. My appointment was for the following day. The ultrasound showed no sign of stones. Since this was inconclusive, my GP and the radiographer agreed that I should get a CT scan. That is when I was told that I had a tumor.

When I went back to my GP (Dr. Debbie Formosa St John) with the results of the ultrasound and the scan, she suggested that I go to Mater Dei again. From the triage, I was sent to the gynaecology ward, and, having been seen by the doctors on duty, it was suggested that I return the following morning for an ultrasound. I returned to Mater Dei hospital the following morning. To cut the long story short, I was hospitalized until Tuesday, December 24, 2019. I had an MRI just before I was discharged. I returned to the hospital on Saturday, December 28, 2019, for pre-op tests and a laparoscopy. The results confirmed the results of the CT scan at Da Vinci hospital: there were signs of peritoneal disease. That was it! Here I was having to face death, having to face the realization that I was mortal, that I was fragile, that I needed help. I had experienced the death of relatives and friends, but facing your own death is completely different. I fell apart. The Kübler-Ross model did not really apply in my case. The five stages of which Kübler-Ross speaks are denial, anger, bargaining, depression (also referred to as preparatory grieving), and acceptance.[16] In my case, there was only confusion: I was an academic with projects, dissertation-supervision duties, multiple articles unfinished, various collaborations with various international people, and so many other responsibilities. I had no children of my own, but my parents were both alive, and I had family and friends, as well as so much unfinished work.

COVID-19 made 2020 the worst year in the life of most people. The social distancing that was required and the social and economic upheaval that took place made our lives almost unbearable. For me, it was my first year of cancer. I started chemotherapy in February of that year. Two chemo sessions later, I was told that the cancer in my uterus had shrunk and that I could have surgery. I had my surgery on April 1, 2020. Two of my most significant life experiences took place on that date: the first one was in 2015 when

I defended my doctorate in Durham, UK. This time it was a total hysterectomy.

Surgeons found two cancers during my surgery: one in the fallopian tube and one in the uterus. My ovaries, my tubes, and my cervix were removed, along with my uterus. After the surgery, I received another four chemo sessions. The treatment with Taxol and Carbo was harsh. I was finished with those at the end of June. But I was still to have five weeks of radiotherapy. This lasted until September of 2020. I was told that there was no trace of cancer at my meeting with the oncologist in mid-November, after a CT scan and an MRI which showed no sign of any cancer cells remaining. I was so glad. I felt that I had had my fair share of pain and suffering in my life, and that I would not have to suffer such physical discomfort again . . .

This is when Tina came into my life. Tina is a Yorkshire terrier. She was born on October 7 and was eight weeks old when I got her. Owning a dog had been on my bucket list. Many times in my life, I had felt a certain sorrow that I would die without ever having owned a dog. I was certain that a human being needs to know a dog at least once in his or her life. The French poet Anatole France is quoted as saying that "until one has loved an animal, a part of one's soul remains unawakened,"[17] and I realized that now was the time to get a dog. Tina has been my bundle of joy.

The good news about my health was short-lived. I was seeing blood again. My doctors soon told me that the cancer was growing again, this time in my vagina. It had now become urgent: I had to write this book. I had to speak about the gaze of the Crucified Christ. I had to tell my story. I had to share the news about Christ's invitation to me to stay where he could see me.

We hide from the face of God all the time. Genesis 3:8–10 tells us about God looking for the first human beings:

> When they heard the sound of the LORD God walking about in the garden at the breezy time of the day, the man and his wife hid themselves from the LORD God among the trees of the garden. The LORD God then called to the man and asked him: Where are you? He answered, "I

heard you in the garden; but I was afraid, because I was naked, so I hid."

I no longer wish to hide from God. On the contrary, I want to be able to gaze into his eyes so that my circumstances become bearable.

The year 2021 was proving to be just as difficult as the previous one. I was being given chemo treatment again. I cried often. Not only because I was getting my second chemo treatment, not only because I had been told clearly and plainly that we can no longer speak of a cure in my case, but because I had doubts as to whether my life had been worth living—that is, whether it had made the world better than it was when I was born. I was feeling real sorrow over all sorts of things. I cried when local priests were accused of pedophilia. I cried when I saw concrete buildings rising all around me; I cried when I realized that the beauty of the Maltese islands was being destroyed by developers. I cried when other cancer patients whom I had encountered on my journey passed away, some of them leaving young families behind.

My friend Francois called me some weeks ago. I told him how sad I was that I would be leaving this world worse than I had found it. Francois told me something that was very consoling. He told me that if I were to follow that principle, I would have to consider Christ as a failure. The only thing that we can hope to do, he said, is to improve the life of someone. To expect to change the world is unrealistic. But to hope to change the life of one person, or of a few, is possible.

I shared my retreat experience with the psychologist at the oncology hospital, and she told me that perhaps I should put myself in the position of Christ on the cross, gazing at the crowd. I too feel like my life is draining away. I too feel the contortions of pain and illness. I too feel the need to ask others to stay where I can see them. I need others to accompany me at my exit. I need to gaze at them and to love them. There will be days when I can no longer serve those around me, but I am hoping that I will be able to always love them, and to be able to gaze lovingly at them.

Endnotes

1. "Vision and Mission," Preca Community, http://precacommunity.org/who-we-are/vision-and-mission/.

2. Keith Micallef, "Attack on Curia in 1984 Benefited Faith in Malta," *Times of Malta*, October 25, 2013, https://timesofmalta.com/articles/view/-Attack-on-Curia-in-1984-benefited-faith-in-Malta-.491950.

3. See John of the Cross, *Dark Night of the Soul*, trans. David Lewis (Charlotte, NC: TAN Classics, 2010). Saint John of the Cross writes about the suffering, the pain, and the torment involved in taking the spiritual life seriously. The dark night that Saint John describes is not abandonment by God but rather a desolation as the soul proceeds towards unity with God. More recently, the "dark night of the soul" has been interpreted more widely to refer to the trials of life and to an experience of God's absence.

4. Mother Teresa, *Come Be My Light: The Private Writings of the Saint of Calcutta*, ed. Brian Kolodiejchuk (New York: Doubleday, 2007).

5. John Eagen, "An Intimate Request," in *Hearts on Fire: Praying with Jesuits*, ed. Michael Harter (Chicago: Loyola Press, 2005), 85. https://issuu.com/loyolapress/docs/hearts_on_fire.

6. A. W. Tozer, *The Pursuit of God*, ed. James L. Synder (Ventura, CA: Regal Books, 2013), 84.

7. G. David Williams, *Under the Gaze of God: Perspectives on Spiritual Development* (self-pub., Xlibris, 2020), back cover.

8. Paul Tillich, "You Are Accepted," in *Model Sermons for Today's Preacher: A Chorus of Witnesses*, eds. Thomas G. Long and Cornelius Plantinga Jr. (Grand Rapids: Eerdmans, 1994), 92–101, esp. 99.

9. Pedro Arrupe, "Fall in Love." Ignatian Spirituality. https://www.ignatianspirituality.com/ignatian-prayer/prayers-by-st-ignatius-and-others/fall-in-love/.

10. "'Late Fragment' by Raymond Carver," Words for the Year, https://wordsfortheyear.com/2014/07/07/late-fragment-by-raymond-carver/.

11. Tozer, "The Gaze of the Soul," in *Pursuit of God*, 79–90.

12. Meister Eckhart, "Sermon Fifty-Seven," in *The Complete Mystical Works*

of Meister Eckhart, trans. and ed. Maurice O'C Walshe (New York: Crossroad, 2009), 295–299, esp. 298. https://philocyclevl.files.wordpress.com/2016/10/meister-eckhart-maurice-o-c-walshe-bernard-mcginn-the-complete-mystical-works-of-meister-eckhart-the-crossroad-publishing-company-2009.pdf.

13. Jasper Hopkins, *Nicholas of Cusa's Dialectical Mysticism: Text, Translation, and Interpretive Study of* De Visione Dei, 3rd ed. (Minneapolis: Arthur J. Banning, 1985), 686, https://jasper-hopkins.info/dialecticalmysticism.pdf.

14. Hans Urs von Balthasar, *Seeing the Form*, vol. 1 of *The Glory of the Lord: A Theological Aesthetics*, trans. Erasmo Leiva-Merikakis, ed. John Riches (Edinburgh: T. & T. Clark, 1982) 329.

15. Abel Giglio and John Formosa, *Venerable George Preca: 1880–1962*, trans. Margaret Mortimer (Marsa, Malta: SDC, 1999), 11–12.

16. "The 5 Stages of Grief," Grief.com, https://grief.com/the-five-stages-of-grief/.

17. Anatole France, Goodreads, https://www.goodreads.com/quotes/4432-until-one-has-loved-an-animal-a-part-of-one-s.